FAITH, FAMILY, AND FORMATION

God's Plan Revealed

"Show me O Lord, Your Way"
(Psalm 27:11)

Dedication

To Mom and Dad

Ted and Connie Morrison

FAITH, FAMILY, AND FORMATION

God's Plan Revealed

ISBN: 978-1-945423-21-5 (Paperback)

Front Cover Artist: Emma Lentz

Book Designed by the International Localization Network Staff

Printed in the United States of America.

First Printing edition 2020 Five Stones Publising

A division of:
The International Localization Network
109 Sunset Court #2
Hamburg, NY 14075

Table of Contents

6

Acknowledgements

Reviewers

Thanks to my four adult children, Lynn Chapman, Tina Hardin, Maria Lentz, and Anthony G. Bonacci, and to my four siblings, Carol Hrynczak, Margaret Armillotti, Joyce Donatelli, and Dennis Morrison, for their review of the manuscript and their helpful contributions and suggestions.

Thanks also to Mrs. Shirley Tornik, friend and parishioner, who reviewed and critiqued the manuscript numerous times.

Artwork

Thanks to my granddaughter, Emma Lentz, a college student in Visual Communications Design, for creating and designing the covers for this book.

Forward

The message for each of us in this book is: God has a plan for my life.

Tony makes real this theological truth. His story gives it flesh and bones and sinews. He makes this truth more real by sharing his life with us.

As you read his life story, you will be moved to ask yourself questions about God's plan for your own life.

Hopefully, you will be brought to the point where you see the effect of past events in your own life on that plan of God. There will come to your mind the great events of your life, both positive and negative. There will also come to mind events which seemed insignificant when they occurred, but, over time, proved to be important factors in that plan of God.

Besides making more real that theological truth of God's plan for your life, Tony's story, from his earliest childhood memories and his beginning school days, through his marriage and graduate degrees, his extended family relations, his professional career and his ministry as a deacon, to the death of his dear wife Elaine and his optimistic outlook to the future will highlight for you two elements of God's life plan for each of us to which we can all relate.

From sharing Tony's life story we can make these two elements more real and alive in our own plan of life. Those two elements are faith and family.

Faith: Again and again in his story, Tony's choices and future were guided by his deep faith. His belief in God was completely integrated into his living of life. Faith totally dominated and formed his life. Life and faith were one and the same. As he himself puts it so succinctly in his reflections: life's purpose, for a person of faith, is to return to God.

Family: Family, in Tony's life, is like an outstandingly bright thread in a woven tapestry. Family weaves itself in and out of practically every facet of Tony's life. Family is for Tony both a rock of stability and, at the same time, a challenge to be confronted.

The story of Tony's Italian family life may seem unique to many of us. The Italian style and traditions of family living may not fit "my" style of family life. Still, the calling to mind of the stability family life gives, and the challenges which family life, even extended family life, presents will cause each of us to pause and reflect on our own family. This reflection will move each of us to ask critical questions about family living in God's plan for my life.

This book is both an interesting and attractive story of one man's life and, at the same time, a thought-provoking read. It is well worth the reader's time.

Bishop Emeritus James A. Griffin, DD, JCL, JD
Diocese of Columbus, Ohio

Preface

For many years, I have said that God connects us with people, places, events, and circumstances via a huge "spider web." That is, the things that happen, the "co-incidences" (really "God-incidences"), and the people who cross and re-cross our path at just the right time, are not random occurrences. They happen under God's perfect control and for a reason. Pope St. John Paul II once said, "In the designs of Providence, there are no mere coincidences." My Dad's story in Chapter X is an example.

In this brief memoir of my physical and spiritual journey, I share my life experiences, demonstrating God's perfect timing and God's control over my personal and professional life. Everything that happens in our life is part of God's plan. Things happen by God's timetable, not ours.

I believe that we fulfill our mission on earth by witnessing God's work in our life to others; our witness may help direct people to Him. We each have a story to tell, a story of faith and a story of encounters with the Lord. Your story or my story could stir someone to seek the Lord or to seek Him more deeply. Perhaps this is the impetus for me to write this book. May my story renew your trust in God's plan for you and bring you closer to Him.

Surely, one way we experience "the kingdom" here on earth is by sharing our "God encounters" with others. It's true, the Kingdom of God is *within* us. It's a way of *being*. It's a way of *acting*. It has to do with trusting God to *run* things and to *judge* things. It has to do with *patience* and *tolerance* – like the patience God has with us.

I was raised in an Italian American family in South Buffalo, New York, the son of Italian immigrants who came to this country as children. My mother liked to tell me the story of how I was born in 1943 "in the hallway" at Buffalo's "Columbus Hospital" because the hospitals were full due to World War II.

Raised in the happy decade of the post-war fifties, when people were buying homes, stoves, refrigerators, and television sets, I was very blessed in spite of losing my biological father at the age of three, and almost losing my "new" Dad at the age of thirteen.

In this memoir, I present my journey of faith with all its blessings, trials, and tribulations. A heart attack at the age of forty-four was one way of God getting my attention. As I share my encounters with God and others, the "milestones" that led me from altar boy to deacon, I witness how God's timing is always perfect.

I've come to believe that our body fades and passes, no matter how hard we try to preserve it. Our "earthen vessels" are meant to teach us to rely on God and not on ourselves. We have a radical dependence on God, a radical trust in God.

It's been said that "God won't give us more than we can handle." I would add, "God will always give us people to help us withstand our toughest trials in life." My journey has had its ups and downs, but the Lord has given me loyal, supportive family and sent friends who cross and re-cross the path of my life at just the right time. I believe that God allows trials in our lives to help us pray, trust, and be grateful for what we have.

And God gives us choices: choices to receive God's messengers, hear them, and heed them; to see Christ in others, and to accept Him; and to choose opportunities for holiness. As many have said, "Holiness is intimate contact with Jesus."

As we mature, we grow in humility. Giving of oneself, a kind of "self-forgetfulness," must come first. Eventually, we come to realize that all that we are and all that we have are gifts from the Lord. It is only by God's grace that we accomplish what we have, or become who we are. We continuously grow spiritually (at "God's speed") perhaps right up to the moment of death.

✝

The Early Years
(Long Term Memories)

Ted and Connie with
Carol and I

"Starting today, you have a new daddy!" Uncle Ralph had a broad smile on his face as he herded my little sister Carol and me into the kitchen. He said, "His name is 'George,' but they call him 'Ted,' and he will take good care of you." Ted had been introduced to my mother "Connie" by Ted's sister-in-law soon after he immigrated to Buffalo in search of work. She told 35-year old Ted, "Look, I insist you meet my friend Connie; she's a widow with two little children."

From the other room in the tiny apartment, we could hear lots of happy chatter as relatives and friends celebrated Mom's marriage to the tall, handsome blue-eyed Canadian man from Cape Breton, Nova Scotia who had served in the Canadian Army Corps of Engineers ("Sappers') during the war.

It was July 19, 1948. I was five; Carol was four. We had lost our Daddy "Carmen" (Italian name "Carmelo") in November, 1946 of a heart attack in his sleep when he was only 39. On Sunday morning, November 17, 1946, Mom tried to wake him for Mass, but he didn't respond. Thinking he was joking, she poked and prodded him. Finally, she called her Mother, Grandma Montalbano into the room; after one look at him and one feel of his wrist, Grandma said, "Call the priest."

Carol and I were too little to remember our Daddy Carmen, but our dear mother Connie (Italian name "Concetta") had told us stories about him. He was born in Soveria Mannelli, Calabria, Italy, and came to this country with his parents Antonio Carmelo and Maria Antonia, and sister Vincenzina when he was eighteen. He had no formal education, but somehow learned the barbering trade in Buffalo.

Carmelo and Parents.

Carmen met my mother "accidentally" when picking up his sister Vincenzina ("Jenny") from a friend's house. The story goes that he came into the house very angry from waiting for his sister Jenny, but my Mom was there, and their eyes met. Suddenly he was not in a hurry anymore. Even though he was eleven years older than Connie, this was the girl for him! They dated and were married in Buffalo on September 12, 1942 (more about that date later).

Knowing that Connie could not afford to buy a wedding dress and veil, Carmen told her she could wear a suit. She said, "Nothing doing, because everyone will gossip." So Carmen bought her a wedding dress and veil but refused to buy her an engagement ring. He did buy her a wedding ring.

They went to Coney Island, New York City, for their honeymoon. Every summer, Carmen would close the barber shop for a day or two during the Erie County Fair and take her there. He loved her dearly, but he was very old-fashioned and would not let Connie wear lipstick, even on their wedding day!

Carmen wanted Connie to let her hair grow long and "Put it in a bun," like his sister. She cut her hair "on the sly," and told him, "Curly hair never grows." Apparently he believed her.

Mom said he was a hard-working man, running his little barber shop in the downstairs of the three story apartment building he owned on South Park Avenue in South Buffalo. She told us how he often asked her to "watch the shop for a minute" while he "needed to go upstairs to fix something in one of the apartments." She would delay the next customer (with Carol and me in tow) as best she could until he returned. Carmen also owned a one acre plot in the suburb of Hamburg, New York, which he dug by hand to grow a lush garden of fresh vegetables, a custom he undoubtedly brought from Italy. Mom also told us that he took us to the beaches on Lake Erie every summer. I don't remember these excursions, but I have old pictures of these times which I treasure.

The very earliest memory I have is walking down South Park Avenue when I was four, with my little arm up in the air. My new

15

daddy-to-be "Ted" was holding my hand as he walked me to pre-school at P.S. # 29, where my teacher was "Mrs. McIntosh." She never knew that the kids called her "Miss Fatty Apple" behind her back. But my Mom and Dad wanted me to have a Catholic education, so off to Holy Family School I went for first through eighth grades.

As I think back on the early years, I realize that my long term memory is acute and accurate, but my short term memory is not. Perhaps the Lord planned it that way for a reason. As we get older, we can better appreciate the blessings of Faith, family, food, and friends that God has given us. And we can better appreciate the people He has brought into our lives who sometimes cross our path more than once.

Sister Gaudentia ("Fusillade")

I quickly learned that things were different at the Catholic school, stricter and more disciplined. The good Sisters of Mercy kept a close eye on our every move. It started with Sister Dionysius in first grade, and continued on through Sister Anne Marie in eighth grade.

Holy Family School

In the second grade, Sister Isidore laid down the law with a slap of her wooden yardstick on her desk, loud enough for us to jump. While she did not hesitate to place a misbehaving boy into the kneehole of her desk, she hand-picked some of the "good boys" to be trained as altar boys. I was proud to be given a plastic card to take home and memorize the Latin responses to the priest at Mass. *"Ad Deum qui laetificat juventutem meam"* ("To God who gives joy to my youth") was the first response to the priest's "*Introibo ad altare Dei*" ("I go unto the altar of God.") as he began Mass. Mom and Dad would read and speak the priest's lines from the plastic card, and I would recite the Latin responses. It was good training that prepared me to serve morning and Sunday Masses with my "partner" Jack Craven until we were seniors in high school. We were assigned to serve for 6:15, 6:45, 7:15, or 7:45 a.m. Mass for a week at a time.

During those years of serving at Mass, I had my first spiritual awakening: was I being called to be a priest? My parents would have been thrilled! When I was about ten years old, Father O'Shea trained me to be a "Master of Ceremonies," a special role of detailed service to the bishop when he came to administer the sacrament of Confirmation. On one such occasion, Father O'Shea introduced me to Bishop Burke, and as I knelt to kiss the bishop's ring (the custom in those days), he looked down at me and in a booming voice said, "Tell me, Anthony, WHEN are you going to enter the seminary?" Not, "Are you thinking about being a priest?" I stammered something like, "Well, Your Excellency (a term we used in those days), I'm not sure..." Perhaps Father O'Shea was disappointed with my answer.

I think I was "The teacher's pet" in third grade, because my teacher (who cried and sobbed when she read us the account of Jesus' passion and death) gave me a lovely statue of Saint Anthony at the end of the school year, a statue I still have on my bedroom dresser. In fourth grade, "Miss Milligan" broke the hearts of every little boy in the class when she announced that she "...would be going away for a few weeks, and when I come back, my name will be 'Mrs. Ryan.'" (Surely, we thought, when we grow up, we will marry her!) Sister Roseanne recognized that the boys and girls of her fifth grade class were beginning to have cases of "puppy love," so she skillfully separated the "couples" as she discovered them.

"You may have heard that I'm mean; well, I am!" declared Sister Michelle on the first day of sixth grade as she slapped the yardstick on her desk. But she taught us well, and instilled in us a respect for all types of authority: civil, religious, and military. Sister Caritas (her name means "Love" in Latin) was a very special seventh grade teacher. Many years later, my dear wife Elaine and I reunited with her at Elaine's 50 year reunion at Mount Mercy Academy, South Buffalo's all-girls' Catholic high school where Sister Caritas taught after her many years at Holy Family Elementary School.

Sister Caritas

The good sisters and lay teachers taught us many prayers, some of which I still recite silently after receiving Holy Communion. My favorite is the one "Miss Milligan" taught us in the fourth grade:

"O my God, I believe in Thee; do Thou strengthen my Faith.

All my hopes are in Thee; do Thou secure them.

I love Thee with all my heart and soul; teach me to love Thee daily more and more.

I am sorry for having offended Thee; do Thou increase my sorrow."

Surely, the Lord is pleased with this child's prayer I have recited for 70 years.

I recall one special day In April of 1957, when Sister Gaudentia, the school principal, rode in the back seat of Dad's 1955 Ford along with Sister Anne Marie, my eighth grade teacher. We were driving across town to Canisius High School, where I was to represent my school in the "Diocesan Spelling Bee." Sitting nervously in the middle of the front bench seat between Mom and Dad, I thought of dozens of words I had been practicing for months with my parent's and the Sisters' help. In the second last round, I erred on the word "fusillade," a word I had never heard before. I was awarded "seventh place" and given a gold medal with a blue and gold ribbon, a memento still in my dresser drawer. The good sisters praised me all the way home, saying that "Anthony had represented Holy Family School very well." I was proud and disappointed at the same time.

My first "job" was doing yard work for "Mrs. Stoop," a widowed lady on the East end of Tifft Street who was a Traveler's Insurance agent. It started with my friend "Bruno" and I shoveling snow for her at the age of ten. Mrs. Stoop called me back in the Spring to plant flowers, weed, sweep her driveway, wash her windows and basement floor, and other miscellaneous jobs. I cut her grass in the summer and raked leaves in the fall. My pay was initially fifty cents per hour, but she gradually increased it to $1 per hour by the time I was in high school. I banked every penny and eventually bought my first car with my savings.

My life-long "best friend" Jack Craven, although a shy boy, was one of the kindest people God ever put in my life. In addition to serving Mass together, we were fellow Boy Scouts of Troop 120 at Holy Family Church. We survived many fishing escapades, either to the shore of Lake Erie on our bikes, or to "South Park Lake," which was really a pond at the Botanical Gardens in Lackawanna.

On one occasion when we were about eight or ten years old, Jack's father and mother rescued us during a soaking rainstorm, the worst part of which was Jack having been stung on the hand by a "bullhead" catfish. He bled so bad, I thought he was going to die! (More about our common experiences later.)

20

One summer, my Mom's cousins from New York City came for a visit. The two young "ladies" were eyeing my Dad and took pictures with their arms around him. While they were downtown shopping and Dad was at work, Aunt Vivian (Mom's sister) and Uncle Ralph came for a visit and found Mom heartbroken and crying over her cousins' flirty behavior. She didn't want the other NYC relatives to see pictures of them with their arms around Dad. Secretly, and unknown to my Mom, Uncle Ralph snuck into their room, unrolled and re-rolled all the rolls of undeveloped film, thus exposing them to the light. Later, a letter arrived from NYC, saying that none of their pictures came out!

On Saturday, May 4, 1957, two husky men in hard hats stood stone-faced at the door of our "new" house on Tifft Street. I had just arrived home from taking the entrance exam for Bishop Timon High School, the all-boys Catholic school on McKinley Parkway. "Is your mother home?" said one of the men. I sensed that something was wrong, because these were not recognizable friends. I called to Mom who was in the basement washing clothes for our family of seven. As she came up the stairs and saw the two men in their hard hats, she turned pale, covered her mouth and muttered, "Oh, God!" Little did we know that Dad had suffered a serious head injury at the steel plant.

As she removed her apron and pulled on an old blue raincoat, she said, "Tony and Carol, feed the kids; your Dad has been hurt and these men are taking me to the hospital; I'll call you…" I shook my head and tried to understand what was happening. Was Dad going to die? Who would take care of us?

My sister Carol, then 12, was thirteen months younger than me, and we now had two younger sisters, Margaret and Joyce, and our little brother Dennis to care for. Mom had left spaghetti sauce on the stove, and I knew how to cook pasta, so I put a big pan of water on the stove to boil.

After what seemed like an eternity, Mom called, crying hysterically, and told me, "Tony, you get the kids down on their

21

knees right now and pray; ask God to let your father live. He's in surgery and they are removing part of his skull which was crushed in the accident. I'll call you back soon. Uncle Ralph and Aunt Vivian are here with me."

We did as she said, praying and crying at the same time. After we said the rosary, I remember shaky so badly with worry that I spilled the pasta in the sink while pouring it into the colander. I went outside to tell Carol, who was taking the garbage out. I said, "Guess what?" She broke down there in the driveway, thinking I was going to tell her that Dad had died. I said, "I spilled the pasta in the sink!" She said, "Oh! That's okay; just spoon it back into the pot!"

When Mom came home, she told us Dad was "critical." We didn't know that meant he could die at any moment. Dad lay in critical condition at Buffalo General Hospital for about two weeks. In the meantime, every class at Holy Family School prayed for his recovery. I took on the responsibility of going to daily Mass and receiving Holy Communion, praying earnestly for Dad to recover.

A week after the accident, Uncle Ralph took me to the hospital to see him. We walked into a "ward," a long room with several dozen beds, and I rushed ahead of Uncle Ralph, looking for my Dad. He was so swollen and bandaged that I walked right past him, not recognizing him. Uncle Ralph pulled me back and pointed, "There's your Dad." I was very shaken as I looked at this man with swollen red cheeks and bandages on his head. I told him I was going to Mass and Holy Communion every day, and he cried, thanking me for being "a good boy."

Dad was permanently disabled since that sad day. Although he tried, he was unable to return to work full time. He had suffered too many injuries, including broken ribs and some loss of memory and mental acuity. Years later, Dad told me about the horrible feeling of defeat he experienced as he walked to Timon High School that fall to put a down payment on my tuition. He had no idea how we would pay for my education, let alone my four younger siblings.

But God provides. Mom and Dad had a friend named Joyce Parks who operated a little delicatessen on South Park Avenue. At this time, Mrs. Parks was getting older and suffering from medical problems. She asked Mom to take over the store, which then provided a meager income for our family. Through long hours and hard work, we survived.

The memories of these elementary years are precious reminders of God at my side no matter the circumstances.

✝

Morrison's Grocery
(Lots of Stories)

Dad never got a big cash settlement from that accident as he might have today, but he kept his sense of humor about his plight. One day, as he was peeling apples for Mom's applesauce, I was complaining that my high school friends were bragging about their father's positions and how much money they made. Dad said, "Oh, yeah, well, tell them that your Dad sits home and peels apples and makes 500 bucks a month!" – his disability pension. "Papa," as we called him, was a gentle and loving soul with a good sense of humor. He will always be remembered for his wit and wisdom.

My mother "Concetta" Montalbano, had immigrated to the United States from Bagheria, Sicily as a seven year old with her mother, sister, and brother in 1925. Her father Nicholas had immigrated earlier and sent them money to come to America. After he passed on, she worked at "Frank's Laundry" on Swan Street in downtown Buffalo to help support her family.

Although Mom achieved only a tenth grade education in this country, she had a good business mind. She instinctively knew how to operate the store. Early in the morning about three times a week, Mom and I would go to "the wholesale house" to buy huge rolls of unsliced cold cuts and cheese, cases of canned goods like Campbell's Soup and Chef Boy-Ar-Dee products, pasta, canned peas, beans, corn, and other dry goods. Then we stopped at "the farmer's market" on Bailey Avenue for produce, and at another wholesale house for boxes of penny candy and candy bars. Beer, pop (soda), bread, milk, potato chips, pretzels, bread, and ice cream were delivered to the store by various drivers each week.

Mom taught Carol and I how to make change and to always tell the customers, "Thank you, please come again." We worked in the store after school, and enjoyed a certain "status" among the

Morrison's Grocery

neighborhood teenagers who stopped by after school for a bottle of "Nehi" pop and a bag of Wise potato chips. In the summer, they enjoyed a 5 cent popsicle or a 10 cent "Drumstick" ice cream cone. Carol and I met quite a few boyfriends and girlfriends in that store!

However, we lost a few of our friends due to accidents - one young man in a motorcycle accident, and two others in car accidents. Their wakes were our first experiences with death, and they left indelible memories of those friends on our minds.

The most memorable thing about "Morrison's Grocery" was the adult customers, including tenants who lived in the four apartments above the store. They tended to tell all their troubles to Mom, and she always listened.

Mom and Dad could have written a book about all the unusual people and circumstances that occurred in those apartments. For example, there was a guy named "Rick," a nice single man who suddenly disappeared off the face of the earth. He had always paid his rent on time, was a dependable employee of a state institution, and seemed friendly with everyone. The unusual thing was that all his belongings were left in his apartment, including his prosthetic arm! Many times, tenants left in the middle of the night owing several weeks' rent, and were never heard from again. Our unpleasant job was to clean up the messes they left, repaint or wallpaper the apartment, and disinfect the kitchen and bathroom.

There were a number of loyal neighborhood customers of the store who would stop in after work for beer, pop, cigarettes, or a few slices of cold cuts for tomorrow's lunch. A number of times, Mom fed the hobos who had jumped off a train in Lackawanna and were walking up South Park Avenue toward downtown Buffalo. "Missus," they would say, "I haven't had anything to eat for two days; can you spare me a sandwich?" Mom would pull out end pieces of the cold cuts which she had saved for them, and say, "Mister, you want mustard on that?" She would open a loaf of bread and make the man a nice thick sandwich, wrap it up in white delicatessen paper, and offer him a bag of chips or pretzels and a soda as well. Mom never turned them away, believing firmly in the Corporal Work of Mercy, "*Feed the hungry.*"

Mr. Kelly, a railroad engineer who stopped by every night, once admonished Mom for feeding the hobos, saying, "Connie, you're a push-over!; see that chalk mark on the front corner of your building? Don't you know they've marked that spot to show other hobos they can get a meal here?" Mr. Kelly offered to remove the chalk mark, but Mom told him to leave the mark there.

Mom taught us that we can't be Christians only in our words; that we are *the body of Christ*: the hands, feet, and lips of Jesus Christ! It's the *service* we offer, the *actions*, that proclaim our love for God! We are called to **act**, to act like a Christian!

27

One night, a young classmate of mine, "Tommy," came to our kitchen door with tears in his eyes and holding a gym bag. He said, "Mrs. Morrison, my Mom threw me out, and I have no place to go." Without a bit of hesitation, Mom said, "O.K., Tommy, you can bunk in with Tony tonight, and we'll talk about it tomorrow." In the morning, she instructed him, "Now go home and tell your mother that you're sorry for what you did or said, and she will forgive you." He did, and they reconciled. We never found out what he had done to anger his mother.

We were taught by Mom's example that we should help the less fortunate whenever the occasion presents itself; that we should treat others as Jesus would treat them. As Pope Francis once said, "It's not about us! It's about selfless giving of *ourselves* for others!"

In my ministry over the years, I have had many opportunities to distribute bread, clothing, and household articles to the needy of the inner city. It's God's work, and I am happy to have the opportunity. (More about this later.)

✝

Sinatra for Lunch
(The paddle)

During my elementary and high school years, I had a persistent sense of insecurity. I worried that when my Mom and Dad were out somewhere in the car, they might not return. I begged to go with them even though they always reassured me that I was capable of taking care of my four siblings, and that I would be safe at home or in the store. I can only guess that those feelings stemmed from the loss of my father Carmen and the near loss of my father Ted.

On one occasion when Mom and Dad were out, I was watching the store when my baby sister Margie was crying and I couldn't stop her. I panicked and called Aunt Vivian, my mother's sister, who immediately got on a bus (she didn't drive) and came to the store, carrying a large glass oven dish with her famous "mille riga" pasta. She quieted baby Margie and kept her eye on the store while I ate the comfort food. Mom and Dad were a little upset that I bothered "Auntie Vivi" (the name Carol and I gave her since we were little).

"Franciscan Friars" and "Timon Gentlemen" were terms we quickly learned as freshmen at the Bishop Timon High School Annex on Como Avenue, a few blocks from the main building on McKinley Parkway. I remember Father Pascal, my Freshman homeroom professor, sweating as he drew pictures of female anatomy on the board, explaining "the facts of life" to us as 13 year- olds. One boy bragged, "Oh, Father, I know all that stuff; my parents already told me."

We "graduated" to the main building for Sophomore year, where we were introduced to more rigorous coursework in math and science. Every lunch hour, "Father Robert" would stroll through the Timon cafeteria with "the Paddle" on his shoulder, singing loudly as he played Frank Sinatra tunes on the P.A. system.

Bishop Timon High School

He was the "Prefect of Discipline," which meant he enforced the rules of dress and behavior for the 400 boys at Bishop Timon High School. He once bragged that he had been a "golden gloves" boxer. We believed it!

"Religion" was always a required course, usually taught by the homeroom teacher. We were so proud when Father Donatus Doino, our Sophomore homeroom teacher, wrote the music and lyrics, and played the piano for the "Timon Fight Song:"

*Lift up the green and the gold, and let the world know the name of
Timon High;*

We've got no banner that's tired and old;

We've got a fresh flag a-flashing in the sky!

We've got tradition, we've got ambition;

We've got the grit that'll make us do or die.

So, lift up the green and the gold,

And let the world know the name of Timon High!

See those Timon Tigers when it's time to fight; Rah!

See them blast into the line like dynamite; Rah!

See them rout their foes, left and right,

See them score another victory!

Rah, Rah, Rah!

*So, lift up the green and the gold, and let the world know the name
of Timon High!*

One day in Religion class, Father Donatus wanted to ease our
fear of Confession (the Sacrament of Reconciliation) for us. As
he reached back into the hood of his Franciscan habit (where the
priests kept detention slips and other paraphernalia), he pulled out
a crisp twenty dollar bill, and said, "I will give this twenty dollar
bill to any boy who can name a sin I haven't heard in confession!"
Mike Booth, the "wise guy" sitting behind me (we were seated in
alphabetical order) shot his hand up in the air, saying, "Father D,
Father D, I know!" Father Donatus said, "O.K. Mr. Booth, name
the sin I've never heard in Confession?" Mike stood up and said
loudly, "Suicide!" Amidst a roar of laughter, he started strutting
forward to collect the twenty, when "Fr. D" said, "Hold it Mr.
Booth!; I've heard attempted suicide in Confession!"

On the last day of Junior year, Father Juvenal Ellis, our chemistry
professor who had prepared us well for taking notes in college, told

High School Friends; Jack, Jim, and I

us to never forget what he then wrote on the board: "Illegitimus non carborundum!" (which translates to "Don't let the bastards grind you down!) Fr. Juvenal also served as the Guidance Counselor, meeting with each boy in our third year to help us select courses for college and a career path.

I well remember my meeting with him, when he said, "Well, Mr. Bonacci, I see you have good grades in chemistry and biology; have you considered the profession of Pharmacy?" Indeed I had, because I had been delivering "orders" (filled prescriptions) to customers' homes for DePotty's Pharmacy for a number of years. I was paid ten cents per order, and the customer usually gave me a quarter or fifty cents.

Once I decided to pursue Pharmacy in college, the Friars of Timon tried to convince me to apply to Fordham University in New York City, because it was a Catholic university that offered Pharmacy. The local Catholic college (Canisius) did not offer it. They told me in no uncertain terms that if I went to the University of Buffalo, I would surely lose my faith, because "they are all atheist professors there."

There was no possibility that I could afford to attend Fordham, so I decided to go to "U.B." in spite of the threat. Having had twelve years of Catholic education, I was confident that my Faith would endure. And it did.

✝

Atheist Professors
(Lose My Faith?)

I was totally naïve as the new Teaching Assistant at U.B. scheduled my courses for my first semester of "pre-Pharmacy." I remember one of his colleagues saying, "Are you crazy? You're scheduling this kid for 18 ½ semester hours!" My registration for Fall, 1961 included Calculus, Chemistry, English, Economics, German, a Pre-Pharmacy course, and R.O.T.C.! My Mom and Dad had always encouraged me to "Get a college education," so I naively accepted his plan.

It was a heavy schedule, but somehow I got through it while working part-time and seeing my girl friend. My long-time friend Jack enrolled for Pre-Pharmacy too, but switched into a Business major several weeks into the first semester.

1959 Simca

Jack was one of my "riders" in my four passenger 1959 Simca sedan which I had purchased from a private owner for $500 the previous summer. My riders paid me fifty cents a day for a two way ride to U.B., and that kept my ten gallon tank full. Of course, gasoline was about $1 per gallon then.

The Air Force R.O.T.C. ("Reserve Officer Training Corps") was mandatory for two years, after which a young man could enlist for the "advanced" R.O.T.C. program for two more years and be assured of a second lieutenant commission upon graduation. We met every Tuesday and Thursday in full uniforms, spit-shined shoes and all. There were classes on Air Force policies and procedures, military strategy, warfare, and the dreaded marching "drills" twice a week on the grassy fields of the University. We often tolerated jeering from various anti-war demonstrators, but largely ignored them, firmly believing that we would defend our country if the need arose.

One day, Jack approached me excitedly and said, "Hey, Ton', have you ever flown?" I said, "No, Jack. I haven't." He said, "Well, guess what, I just signed us up for a flight; we're going to get a free trip to Wright Patterson Air Force Base in Ohio!" At first, I was angry and shocked, but I went. The Air Force, of course, was trying to recruit us for the "advanced" program, so they put us up in "V.O.Q." (Visitor Officers' Quarters), fed us the best food, and indoctrinated us heavily during our two day weekend stay. We flew from Niagara Falls Air Force Base to Fairborn, Ohio on a DC-3 "Gooney Bird" after receiving a *brief* instruction on using the parachute we were obliged to wear during the flight! Neither Jack nor I took the "advanced" R.O.T.C. program.

During one of our snowy trips to U.B., I was engaging the clutch on my Simca when the pedal went limply to the floor. I coasted to a stop, and announced to my riders, "There's something wrong." Jack, in his R.O.T.C. uniform that day, crawled under the car and yelled out, "Do you have a wire coat hanger in the car?" Luckily I did. He bent the wire, broke off a piece, and re-connected the clutch pedal linkage. "Try it now," he yelled. It worked fine and we were on our way. That wired connection was still on the car when I sold it four years later!

34

I told these stories and the "fish story" about Jack at his funeral Mass several years ago, when I had the honor and privilege of assisting as Deacon for the funeral Mass. I miss him greatly.

Elaine Mary Ridder came into my life as a "blind date" on December 7, 1961, just before Christmas of my Freshman year. It was her "Ring Dance," at which time the Seniors at Mount Mercy Academy received their Senior Class rings. (As I recall, it was my friend Jack and his date "Kathy" who fixed us up for the date.) Little did I know, that would be the beginning of a five-year dating

Elaine and Parents - Our First Date

relationship, an engagement, and a marriage that would last 53 years, including four children and eight grandchildren.

After two years of "pre-Pharmacy" courses, I entered Pharmacy School, which proved to be a rigorous three-year marathon of lectures, labs, copious note-taking, exams, and all-night study sessions. Many of us joined a fraternity to have a few hours of fellowship away from the maddening schedule. Following the lead of my life-long friend "Alex," who I had known since kindergarten, I joined the Beta Phi Sigma Pharmacy Fraternity in my Junior year. That fraternity claimed to be "the oldest Pharmacy fraternity in the country." In any case, it offered other "bonuses," such as a complete file of old exams from Pharmacy courses, which were excellent to study from, as many professors repeated the same questions year after year.

We were guilty of a few stunts as fraternity pledges, not the least of which was the smearing of limburger cheese all over an upperclassman's car the night before the annual fraternity "dinner dance" as retaliation for his assigning us ridiculous pledge tasks. I remember us asking him, "Hey, Steve, how's your car running?" when he and his date entered the dance. He wasn't a happy camper.

I clearly remember being in Pharmacy lab on November 22, 1963, when Dr. Lockie came in and told us that President Kennedy had been assassinated. He told us to "pack everything away and go home." On that Sunday morning, I was watching TV at home when Jack Ruby shot Lee Harvey Oswald, the president's assassin. It was a sad time for all Americans, and even more so for us as Catholics, because President Kennedy was our first Catholic president and he was our hero.

The threat of all those "atheist professors" never really materialized, although a few were obvious in elective courses in philosophy, ethics, and some language courses. Some of the professors we encountered were memorable for their repeated maxims, such as "Dr. Spencer" in Bacteriology repeating ad nauseam, 'KEEP YOUR EYE ON THE BACTERIA!" Or, Dr. Taube, our German professor, repeatedly calling us "Kiddos."

Other college acquaintances became life-long friends who maintain contact to this day. "Jerry," a pre-Dent student who took many courses with the pre-Pharmacy group, and his Pharmacy student girl friend "Sue" often double-dated with Elaine and I. Jerry and I especially remember taking a one-year course in Physics as a twelve week accelerated program in the summer between our Freshmen and Sophomore year in order to avoid taking three sciences in the Fall.

I didn't "lose my faith" in college, as some did, but that was probably due to the excellent upbringing by my parents, teachers, and extended family. My parents persevered through many hardships and obstacles, and even with limited resources, they made sure we had everything we needed, including a safe and loving home. I

Life-Long Friend Alex and I
remember Mom buying our first Remington typewriter from a door-to-door salesman for "$1.00 per week" so that we would "be ready for college." It took two years to pay for that typewriter.

Most of all, our parents showed us what a loving marriage looked like. They guided us with their words and actions. We listened, we watched and we learned.

Mom told us we could "do anything we put our mind to if we had a well thought out plan, and if we worked hard (ethically) to accomplish our goal." She spoke from experience. Dad taught us that "our good name is our most valuable asset, and that we must strive to preserve it throughout our lifetime." Dad, too, spoke from experience. He was a man of integrity.

Through college, I continued Sunday worship (and sometimes daily Mass during trying times) in my home parish no matter how busy I was. God was by my side through all five years at the "atheist" school.

✝

Pasta on Sunday
(The Relatives)

The delicious aroma of spaghetti sauce ("sugo") wandered through the house and into my bedroom as I woke. "It must be Sunday," I thought. The familiar sound of sausage and meatballs sizzling in the frying pan and Mom's humming or softly singing accompanied the lovely aroma. "Pasta on Sunday" was one of the traditions of my Italian heritage, which included Mom's thick Sicilian style pizza; Aunt Vivian's beautiful cakes for every birthday, First Communion, Confirmation, Graduation, or Anniversary; Mom's homemade ravioli at Christmas, Aunt Jenny's Easter bread with colored eggs on top ("pupa con uova"), deep fried calamari (squid) "for luck" on New Year's Eve; and, of course, piano or accordion music performed by my twin cousins "Bud" and Nick. After every meal, we kids were repeatedly told, "Wipe-a-da-moos-oo," meaning, "Wipe your mouth."

Mom, Aunt Vivian, and Aunt Jenny would be standing around the kitchen table, jabbering in Italian about ingredients or cooking techniques, and saying they shouldn't eat the special dishes because they'd "get too fat," or because their "corsets were too tight." Dad, Uncle Ralph, and Uncle Mike would be sitting in "the parlor," drinking a beer, and talking about the current work situation at the steel plant.

Some Sundays, I was a guest at Aunt Vivian's house because my twin cousins, Bud and Nick, and their brother Philip were like brothers to me. We played together daily, because in those days,

39

cousins lived just down the block. They taught me how to throw a baseball and a football and how to ride a bike. Our aunts and uncles were just like parents to us. They were expected to correct or discipline us just as readily as our own parents.

Cousins Bud and Nick and I

There were Sunday picnics at Chestnut Ridge Park, and in keeping with tradition, Mom and Aunt Vivian brought cooked pasta, carefully packed in heavy pans wrapped with thick towels to keep it warm. On my birthday one year, they brought homemade pizza and put candles on top for the singing!

Many times, my aunts and uncles told us stories of coming to America on "the big-a boat." We heard about the Papa coming first, to get a job so he could send money for the rest of his family to come to the "United-a-States." We heard of their tough times working menial labor or janitorial/housekeeping jobs; going through the Great Depression of the thirties, eating fried potato or bean sandwiches; taking in laundry or sewing jobs to make a few dollars; and suffering discrimination against Italians, being called "WOP'S" or "DAGOS."

Aunt Vivian (my mother's sister) was a talented seamstress who sewed, crocheted, and knitted. During the Great Depression, she used her talent to make a few dollars to help support her family.

Aunt Vivian and Uncle Ralph

She also took in laundry from more affluent people. Years later, when Elaine and I were newlyweds, she spent many hours custom-making "Early American" style slip covers for the old furniture in our tiny attic apartment. All our relatives remember gifts of her delicate crocheted doilies which were ceremoniously pinned on the arms of every chair and couch.

Uncle Ralph (her husband, who looked like Groucho Marx) was born in Utica, New York. He was a strict disciplinarian who could be very sarcastic at times. We accepted his manner and felt sorry for him when his twin sons joined the U.S. Navy immediately out of high school. In fact, he was so lonely and missed them so much, he would often call me and offer to take me to the Buffalo Bisons' baseball game or to the local bowling alley. He would always say I was "his favorite nephew." One day I realized I was his *only* nephew!

Aunt Jenny ("Vincenzina" in Italian), my father Carmen's sister, and her husband Uncle Mike were from Soveria Mannelli, Calabria, Italy, the birth place of my biological father Carmen. They had no children, so they treated my sister Carol and me as their "children." Aunt Jenny had a very strong personality, but was very generous to us, taking us to "down-a-town" Buffalo on the street car to buy us nice clothes so she could show us off to her "coozins" on the West side. Uncle Mike was very proud of his Kaiser Frazer automobile,

41

so much so that he kept it in the garage covered by a sheet, and only took it out to go visit the "coozins" in Olean or Salamanca, New York. He rode the bus to the Republic Steel plant every day because he didn't want to get ore dust on the car.

The best memories of Aunt Jenny and Uncle Mike include their back-yard "veg-a-table" garden and their making of homemade wine every year. Each fall, they made two *barrels* in their "base-a-ment," some to drink, and some to give away to the "paisani" who came to visit. It took 40 cases of grapes for each barrel - 35 cases of white California grapes for flavor, and about 5 cases of red grapes for color. They bought the grapes at the "farmers' market" on Bailey avenue, always with Aunt Jenny loudly dickering the price with the farmer, and convincing him to deliver the grapes to "my-a house on Tifft-a-Street."

Aunt Jenny and Uncle Mike

I now appreciate how rich and honest is my Italian heritage: the blend of music and singing, laughter and conversation, facial expressions and hand gestures, and frequent displays of emotion.

When I was a child, I was embarrassed by these outward signs, but now I treasure them greatly, because they taught me to be a sensitive person. While that can be a weakness at times, it can also be a strength. For every time that I loudly blurt out my anger or frustration, there is another time that I find myself perceiving another's feelings or empathizing with his or her problems. It has been a valuable asset in my ministry.

In December, 1988, Elaine and I travelled to Baton Rouge, Louisiana for the wedding of my cousin Nick's son (Nick Jr.) to his college sweetheart Diane. It was a beautiful ceremony held in the chapel on the L.S.U. campus.

Fast forward to a Monday morning in November, 1989: I received a call at work from cousin Nick with the tragic news, "Diane is dead." She was travelling home from her father's ("Doc Upp's") house when someone threw a rock from an overpass through her windshield; she was killed instantly.

The young boys who did it weren't apprehended immediately, but after the tragedy was publicized state-wide, they were arrested. Diane's funeral was held in the same chapel where she had been married only eleven months before.

Doc Upp met with the boys several times while they were in custody and over time, reconsidered his hate, anger, and judgement, seeing them as "ordinary boys." At the hearing some months later, the judge asked Diane's father how he should sentence the boys. Doc Upp, who had only recently lost his wife, said that his daughter's life was now lost, but he forgave the boys for their immature choice of dangerous entertainment, "...why should two more lives be lost?" The boys were given parole and civic duties to perform. Doc Upp's story of forgiveness was published in the *Guideposts* magazine in March, 1992. It is a story about a father's love, a story about judging others, and a story about letting God be God.

Doc Upp was not foolish to forgive, as some people said at the time; he knew that God's mercy far exceeds human ideas of mercy. He liked to quote Diane's favorite scripture: "Remember, the Lord forgave you, so you must forgive others." [Col. 3:13] We are challenged to forgive as our Father forgives us.

On August 29, 2005, my 56 year old cousin Philip was a patient at Charity Hospital in New Orleans being treated for "Lou Gehrig's disease" when Hurricane Katrina hit. Since birth, he had struggled with physical limitations, including epilepsy, a speech impediment, and vision problems. Although he received physical, medical, and speech therapy, he had limitations in education and employment. Over the years, his older brothers Bud and Nick hired him to work

Cousin Philip

in their restaurants so that he was able to earn a living for himself.

I would call Philip "a humble servant," because he was never bitter, angry, or complaining about his lot in life, in fact, he gave all of his free time to ministering to the elderly of his apartment complex. Philip visited folks, took them to appointments, shopped for them, and helped them to pay bills and run errands. He accepted and helped others, even though *he* was often not accepted.

After *nine days* of the storm, he was finally rescued by boat and then by helicopter, and returned to a nursing home in Baton Rouge. When I finally reached him by phone, he said, "I made it, cousin Tony; I made it through the storm!" He passed peacefully in a nursing home in 2014.

When I was raising my children, I tried to pass on the stories about my relatives, the meaningful traditions and ancestral language, the foods and customs, because they are a link with our loved ones who have gone before us. As I matured, I experienced other more dormant signs of my heritage which have become a part of me: hand gestures, emotional reactions to good news or bad, Italian words and sayings... perhaps that is just a part of God's great plan, a way to link the present with the past and with the future. Now, on some Sunday afternoons, I cherish the moment when one of my children says, "Come on over, Dad, and have a dish of pasta."

✝

I Do
(All Day Long)

Two weeks after I met Elaine, I panicked when I suddenly realized I needed to get her a Christmas gift. So I did as any panicking young man would do - I went to Mom for help. She said, "Get into the car, and we'll go to the Catholic Store on Broadway." I immediately said, "Oh, Ma, please, I just met the girl; I don't want to get her a religious gift! I'm not going to marry the girl!" We went anyway.

Mom quickly spotted a plastic Blessed Mother statue on the shelf behind the checkout counter. It was a night light, music box, and jewelry box all rolled into one. She said, "Any nice Catholic girl would love it! We'll take it!" I gave the statue to my new girlfriend, Elaine Mary Ridder, that Christmas of 1961, and it has served us well. It still sits on my bedroom dresser, having seen us through 53 years of marriage, four children and eight grandchildren, the passing of our parents and other relatives, several job changes and moves, and more than a few serious medical issues.

Elaine was my "steady" through five years of college. We typically dated on Saturday night, when her father Herman would be sitting on the front porch, even in the winter, watching through the window Jackie Gleason's "The Honeymooners" show on TV. Herman was a WW I veteran and had served in the Gas Corps.; as a result, he had serious breathing problems and emphysema. He always called me "kid." I'm sorry he didn't live to see us married or to enjoy his grandchildren.

Blessed Mother Statue

When Herman passed on February 12, 1964, my Mom and Dad respectfully attended the wake because they had known him as the neighborhood plumber, and because "Tony has been dating this girl for a few years now." When Mom sat next to Elaine's mother Margaret at the visitation, she expressed her sympathy and asked, "Margaret, what year were you and Herman married?" Margaret replied, "1942." Mom said, "Hmm, Carmen and I were married that year." She then asked what month. Margaret replied, "September," Mom said, "Hmm, Carmen and I were married in September." She then asked what date in September. Margaret replied, "September 12." Mom exclaimed, "My goodness, Margaret, we were married on the same day!" So Elaine's folks and mine were married on the same day in the same year, in the same city! "September 12" was very special to us all our married life, and as it turned out, we moved into our home in Plain City seven years later on September 12!

During my college years, we often went on "cheap dates" such as picnics at the park or trips to the beach on Lake Erie. Elaine worked full time at the telephone company as a long distance operator and part time in a department store. She had off on Wednesdays. I worked part time at Our Lady of Victory Hospital, a job I inherited from a graduate student I knew at U.B., and I had off on Wednesday afternoons. We took advantage of this schedule, and had many pleasant dates at the zoo, at a museum, or at a movie. During this time, I decided that *hospital* pharmacy, *not* retail, was the profession for me.

I "pinned" Elaine with my fraternity pin (a kind of pre-engagement) during the fourth year of my five-year Pharmacy program. At Christmas time of my fifth year I "popped the question" and she said "yes." We immediately began to plan our wedding for the following June.

Coming from an Italian family, it would of course be a big wedding! I was honored to have my twin cousins Bud and Nick in the wedding party, as well as my friend Eddie and my brother-in-law Walter. I asked Bud to be my best man, as I had been his best man a few years earlier. What I remember most of that day (June 18, 1966) is that view from the altar, looking down the aisle and seeing the most beautiful girl in the world walking toward me.

I also remember one "glitch" that occurred when folks were arriving at church. My mother and my Aunt Jenny had been "on the outs" for months before (typical for Italian women), and Mom didn't know that we had invited Aunt Jenny. I was standing in the vestibule of the church with Mom when Aunt Jenny walked in. At first, they glared at one another, but after a few minutes, they both started to cry and hugged, forgetting what they were angry about. It's often been said that "forgiveness is the most perfect form of love."

We had a breakfast for immediate family at a local restaurant, and a few hours later, a lunch for family and the out-of-towners at the "Swiss Chalet" restaurant in downtown Buffalo. In the early

Our Wedding June 18th 1966

evening, we hosted a reception for over 500 people at the local Steelworkers' Union hall, which we had rented for $50. There was a live orchestra and tons of food, mostly homemade by the relatives. Elaine's cousin Dick was the bartender for an open bar.

We honeymooned for a few days at the "Thousand Islands," North of Syracuse, New York, then crossed into Canada, and travelled North along the Saint Lawrence Seaway in my 1965 Volkswagon to Montreal, Quebec City, and the St. Anne deBeaupre Shrine. On the return, we drove through upstate New York, stopping at Lake Champlain and Lake George in the Catskills.

During our first married year, we had five paychecks coming in: I worked full time as a pharmacist at Our Lady of Victory Hospital, moonlighted at DePotty's Pharmacy two nights a week, and taught a Pharmacy lab one afternoon a week at U.B. Elaine worked full time as a long-distance operator for the telephone company and moonlighted evenings and weekends at Hens and Kelly department store in downtown Buffalo.

A few months after we were married, I received a Draft notice to appear for a physical exam and possible induction for service, as the Vietnam War was raging at that time. However, about the same time, we found out that Elaine was pregnant, so my Draft Board re-classified me as "IV-A," meaning I would only be called up after all single men and married men with no children.

We were determined for me to attend graduate school (somewhere) for a Master of Science degree in hospital pharmacy. During my fifth year at U.B., my Dean, Dr. Michael Schwartz, had stopped me in the hall one day, and advised me to "Look up Clif Latiolais - he's a famous leader in hospital pharmacy. He's at Ohio State University." I did so, and I have always felt that my Dean was one of God's messengers directing my path toward my career in hospital pharmacy.

✝

The Big E
(Big Shot in Graduate School)

We had learned that our first child was due in July of 1967, so we continued our five jobs and saved every penny we could. In the Fall of 1966, I flew to Columbus to interview for graduate school at O.S.U. The only time I could go was on a Friday night, as I had to be back to work at O.L.V. hospital by Sunday morning. I was so impressed that Dr. Clifton Latiolais, Director of Pharmacy at the hospital, and College of Pharmacy Dean Lloyd Parks came in on a Saturday morning, in suits and ties, to interview a 23 year old kid from Buffalo! They were gracious and welcoming, as were the current graduate students who put me up for the night.

Several months later, after submitting my academic records, I received word that I was accepted to the graduate school, but I didn't realize that I had not yet received acceptance to a "Residency" in Hospital Pharmacy at one of the participating hospitals. My life-long Buffalo friend Alex, who was also an applicant to the same program, informed me that he had received a residency offer from the O.S.U. hospital. I immediately completed the necessary paperwork, and was offered a residency at O.S.U. hospital.

My Dad and I traveled to Columbus in the Spring of 1967 to rent an apartment and purchase a stove, refrigerator, and some furniture. The plan was for Elaine to stay in Buffalo until our baby was born. Dad was very unhappy that I had to pay $87.50/month when our apartment in Buffalo had been $65/month!

I walked into the hospital to begin my graduate and residency program on July 1, 1967, my 24th birthday. Unfortunately, I got a $20 parking ticket that first day because I parked too close to a corner on a side street about ten blocks from the hospital. I didn't know about University "Parking Permits."

College of Pharmacy O.S.U

As Pharmacy "Residents," we were classified as "Graduate Research Associates," which qualified us to receive a whopping stipend of $300/month (tax-free). But the real benefit was the waiver of graduate school tuition and fees! We were obligated to spend 20 hours per week working in assigned areas of the hospital pharmacy, while simultaneously taking rigorous graduate courses such as biostatistics, business organization, and personnel and financial management. To top it off, we had to do bench research with a Pharmacy faculty member and write a thesis to qualify for the Master's degree.

Fourteen days after I began the program, I made the trip to Buffalo just in time for the birth of our first child, Lynn Marie. Fourteen days later, Elaine flew to Columbus on Mohawk Airlines, experiencing air travel for the first time in her life. I fondly remember her coming down the stairs of the little aircraft onto the tarmac with 14-day old baby Lynn wrapped in four blankets because "we have to keep the baby warm." Baby Lynn got a heat rash as a result.

I took Elaine to Blendon Woods Park even before taking her to our new apartment. I was so excited to show her our new home city! When we arrived at the apartment and she saw the furniture and new appliances, she cried. We were a happy young married couple, on our own in a strange city where we knew no one.

Dr. Latiolais, my mentor, was internationally known as an innovator and leader in hospital pharmacy. In courses and staff meetings, he espoused "The Big E," meaning *excellence* was expected in all our work! He also espoused another "Big E," *enthusiasm*, explaining that the root word here was "*Theo*," referring to God. In fact, the word "enthusiasm" means "in God." We were to use our God-given talents to further our profession and help our fellow man. I never forgot those words, and years later, as a Director of Pharmacy and as a Pharmacy Dean, I did my best to contribute to my fellow man through my profession.

Dr. Clifton J. Latiolais

We felt like "big shots" in graduate school, and jokingly called one of the O.S.U. buildings (Hagerty Hall) "Hagerty High School," because we considered ourselves a step above the undergraduate students. Nevertheless, we had to take some courses on the main campus, including computer programming ("Main Frames" were the cutting edge computers at that time) and journalism (a scientific writing course). We didn't have time for, or interest in, the campus demonstrations and foolishness on "the Oval" which were part of the tumultuous sixties.

I was fortunate to have Dr. Lester Mitscher and Dr. Ted Sokoloski as my advisors for my bench research on the stereochemistry (the molecular shape) of the tetracycline antibiotics. Feeling sorry for myself that first Christmas because we couldn't go home for the holiday, I spent all my free time in the laboratory. I especially remember Dr. Mitscher's excitement when a huge crate arrived from Japan, the $65,000 "Jasko" spectrophotometer instrument that would be my daily workhorse for the next two years. He taught me well, and had the patience of Job when I didn't calibrate the instrument correctly or accidentally broke a "cuvette," the little glass tube that contained the sample we were investigating. During my research and after I completed my thesis, we published several papers on the results of my research.

Other Pharmacy faculty were a great influence on my development. One was a farm boy from Kansas who worked his way through school, all the way to a Ph.D. and professorship in Pharmacognasy (the study of medicinals from plants) and to the position of Associate Dean. A humble man, he lead the prayer of invocation at every college function, and in spite of his position, he insisted that everyone, including students, simply call him "Jack."

I learned that real *humility* is not putting ourselves down or denying our achievements. Real humility is acknowledging our dignity as children of God. It's pride coated with *gratitude*. It's sharing credit for our achievements with God and with others. It's saying, "Yes, God's been good to me," or "I am truly blessed."

As graduate students, we were interested in O.S.U. football, and we could purchase tickets for about $35 for the entire home season! Most of us were newly married and had little spending money, but in those days, we could enter the stadium with picnic baskets loaded with home-fried chicken, beverages, and snacks. Our seats were typically on the 30 or 40 yard line in "C deck" (top of the stadium). If we had babies at home (most of us did), we had to hire a baby-sitter for the entire day, as we went to the BDBITL (band's) "skull session" before the game, and partied after the game.

Dr. Latiolais' program was probably the best M.Sc./Pharmacy Residency program in the country, but he wisely arranged for us to visit similar graduate programs during our two years at O.S.U. We were not "spies," but there was a friendly rivalry among the pharmacy departments of the large teaching hospitals *"around the country,"* as Clif liked to say. His other memorable phrases were, *"first class,"* and *"top flight,"* referring to the quality of service he strove for and expected from his staff and residents. During his years at O.S.U. hospital, he served as president of many local, national, and international pharmacy organizations. We were proud of his accomplishments and proud to be his students and colleagues.

His innovations included an advanced "Unit Dose" drug distribution and administration system, intravenous admixture services, drug information services, and clinical pharmacy practice. Dr. Latiolais prepared and encouraged his pharmacy residents to take on Director of Pharmacy positions at major teaching hospitals upon graduation, and most did so. He traveled extensively, and brought his knowledge and techniques to hospital pharmacists throughout the United States and Canada. I was honored to be part of his "team" for some of those seminars.

Some years later, when I visited him at home during his last days with metastatic prostate cancer, his only regret was that "…I should have gone in sooner," that is, sought treatment sooner. I value those last few visits with one of the most influential people in my life, a man with whom I worked and traveled. His legacy lives on through many of his students and colleagues *"around the country."*

✝

The Bag Show
("Police Shoes")

My classmate Alex and I were fortunate to secure Assistant Director positions with Dr. Latiolais at The Ohio State University Hospitals upon graduation from the M.Sc./Residency program. The Associate Director of Pharmacy continued his role, and the three previous Assistant Directors moved on to Director of Pharmacy positions in other teaching hospitals, including Grant Hospital in Columbus, The University of Kansas Medical Center in Kansas City, Kansas, and Good Samaritan Hospital in Phoenix, Arizona.

Alex and I were assigned responsibility for various "divisions" in the Department of Pharmacy, which at that time had about 90 pharmacists and over 100 pharmacy technicians. We also had responsibility for the Central Sterile Supply (C.S.S.) Department, which provided sterile gowns, instruments, and utensils for medical and surgical areas. We fully supported Dr. Latiolais' innovations in pharmacy services and worked hard to implement them. In addition to the pharmacy services mentioned previously, we operated a large "Manufacturing" section that formulated and assayed various solutions, suspensions, and emulsions. My initial responsibilities were for the Central Sterile Supply, Sterile Products, and Assay and Quality Control areas.

During my first year as an Assistant Director, Dr. Latiolais developed a seminar program for area hospital pharmacists specifically to teach them how to prepare "intravenous admixtures," i.e., sterile drugs added to sterile intravenous solutions, as a pharmacy service to the nursing staff. Up to that time, nurses would prepare the admixtures on the nursing unit, which was a time-consuming task performed in a non-sterile environment. Also, the nurses were often not aware of possible chemical incompatibilities of some combinations of intravenous medications, nor the dosage calculations involved.

Since our nurses were delighted with this service, and since we could prepare these admixtures in a "Laminar Flow Hood," (a special aseptic environment), Dr. Latiolais decided to train other hospital pharmacists to offer this innovative service in their hospitals. These techniques were not being taught in Colleges of Pharmacy at that time.

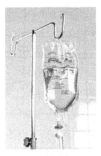

Intravenous Solution Bag

The first "Intravenous Admixture Seminar," November 4-5, 1969, in Columbus, was sponsored by a large intravenous solution manufacturer, and was a great success. That fall, Dr. Latiolais asked me to be part of a team of six men who would put on the program in various parts of the United States and Canada. I was very fortunate to join him and four other colleagues on trips to major American and Canadian cities over the next four years. The two day program, which we came to call "The Bag Show" (because we were introducing plastic I.V. bags at the same time) was a major contribution to improving professional hospital pharmacy services in hundreds of hospitals. One "drawback," as Clif would warn us, was that "You'll have to work twice as hard before we go away, and twice as hard when you get back." That proved to be very true.

The seminars gave me the opportunity to develop my speaking and teaching ability, which I find helpful to this day as I preach or teach in my parish. However, being thousands of miles away from home for a week at a time, with small children at home, presented other challenges. Loneliness took root, and it seemed that every time I was away from home, some appliance would break down at home or the car would start making funny noises.

On one occasion, some of the "company boys" brought several young "ladies" to our hotel room after dinner to offer their services. We were not interested, but one "lady" took one look at my black wing-tipped shoes and said, "Those look like police shoes!" and she promptly left the room with one of the company boys. I'm not proud of those times of over-eating and drinking, but with God's help, I was never unfaithful to my wife.

On one trip, I found God in Boston! There, I met a man named "Ed," a Regional Manager for the sponsoring company. We were having dinner after we set up for the seminar, and as we got to know each other, we talked about our families and shared some pictures. Ed said, "You know, Tony, I really look forward to taking my family to church every Sunday. When I go to church with my wife and kids, it "transcends" everything else. It goes above and beyond my company, my job, my possessions, my worries... I really look forward to prayer and fellowship with other Christians... to the nourishment I receive from the Eucharist and from the Word."

This man had *zeal* for God's house, for God's temple. He showed *eagerness* to be in God's house. His witness to me, his sincere sharing from his heart, showed me that he himself was a "temple of God."

In September of 1970, our second daughter Tina Marie was born at Riverside Hospital in Columbus. I was fortunate to be home and not on one of the "Bag Show" trips when she was born.

✝

Director!
("Lord, Keep Me Going")

In October, 1973, after four years as an Assistant Director of Pharmacy at The Ohio State University Hospitals, one of our previous Assistant Directors offered me an interview with a new hospital pharmacy management company. He had become a Vice President of that company, and they had just secured a contract with Mount Carmel Medical Center to provide contract pharmacy services to that hospital. The former Director of Pharmacy there, a religious sister of the Holy Cross order, was retiring.

I interviewed with the President and Vice Presidents of the company and was offered the position of Director of Pharmacy for Mount Carmel Medical Center. I had interviewed for director positions at several other hospitals, but really wished to stay in Columbus, as we then had two young girls, ages six and three, and had purchased our home in Plain City, Ohio two years previously.

The pharmacy department at Mount Carmel was seriously out of date and needed extensive modernization of services as well as physical renovation. I embraced this new job as "Director" with great enthusiasm, working long hours day and night to provide the patients and medical and nursing staffs with updated pharmacy services. I remembered and tried to emulate my preceptor's *Big E* as I worked with company personnel and pharmacy staff.

During my four years at Mount Carmel, I was able to continue a part-time faculty position in the College of Pharmacy which I truly enjoyed. With several other hospital pharmacy directors in Columbus, I team-taught a "Professional Practice" course to Seniors.

I was fortunate to hire as my Assistant Director a recent graduate of the M.Sc./Residency program from Riverside Hospital. We worked well together, implementing modern services and starting our own Pharmacy Residency program.

During this time, our third daughter, Maria Margaret, was born at Mount Carmel. Also, the pharmacy management company secured a contract to provide pharmacy services to the new "Mount Carmel East Hospital" as well as contracts for pharmacy services at several hospitals in Galion, Bucyrus, and Crestline, Ohio. I assisted in recruiting and orienting pharmacy directors for these new accounts and overseeing their departments.

My mother had been diagnosed with oral cancer on Good Friday, 1972, while I was still at O.S.U., and she was being treated at Roswell Memorial Cancer Hospital in Buffalo while I was at Mount Carmel. She underwent several surgeries, followed by radiation and chemotherapy with an investigational drug called "Cis-D-D platinum," which later became an approved drug for certain cancers. We made as many trips to Buffalo as we could over the next five years (1972-1977).

I especially remember one trip in the Spring of 1977 when Mom was able to wave at our three little girls from her hospital window as they stood downstairs in the parking lot. During that visit, we attended Mass at "Holy Family," the home parish where we grew up. Mom was in great pain as the cancer had spread to the sternum, the breast bone in the center of the chest. I remember praying, "Dear God, if it's your holy and perfect will, please take her home, because we can't stand to see her suffer any more." He called her home on July 12, 1977.

When we returned to Columbus from her funeral, I picked up the Sunday paper and was shocked to see a huge block ad for "Director of Pharmacy, Mount Carmel Medical Center." The new hospital administrator had decided not to renew our contract pharmacy services for the next year, and planned to bring in his own pharmacy director. The pharmacy management company was assured that the hospital was very pleased with our services, but thought they could continue the pharmacy services we had implemented less expensively. I was asked by the company to continue my oversight at the other contract hospital pharmacies and help secure new accounts.

One day before I left Mount Carmel (October 14, 1977), Sister Mary Laurent, a "Pastoral Care" nun who daily visited the patients, came to my office and gave me a hand-painted rock with little flowers and the inscription, "Lord, Keep Me Going." I still have the inspiring rock on my desk at home.

Lord, Keep Me Going

I visited our other accounts for several months, and even though I had a company car and an expense account, I decided this was not the kind of practice I wished to continue. I still had my part-time position at the College of Pharmacy, so I spoke to the retiring Dean about my situation. He was the same man who had recruited me for graduate school, and he was concerned for me. He urged me to continue my part-time faculty position.

As it happened, I was walking on campus that same day when I ran into a faculty member who had taught my graduate course in "Radiopharmaceuticals" (radioactive drugs used for diagnosis or treatment). He had heard of my plight, and he informed me that the new incoming Dean was lying in Riverside Hospital with a

Assistant Dean, 1981

broken arm due to an accident. He advised me to talk to him, because two of his Assistant Dean positions were recently vacant, one due to a death, and one due to a move to another university.

I visited the new Dean in the hospital and explained my situation. He knew of my administrative and scientific background, and said, "Let's talk." After several interviews, I was offered a position in the college office as "Administrative Manager." Over the next few years, the Dean expanded my administrative duties to include fiscal and physical facilities management, and eventually in November, 1981, he promoted me to Assistant Dean. We worked very well together for eleven years.

To the faculty, I was "a known quantity," as they knew me from my graduate school research and my positions at O.S.U. and Mount Carmel hospitals. I tried to be helpful to them by monitoring their research grants and handling their personnel and equipment needs.

On September 29, 1987, I was sitting at my desk, gulping down a sandwich while doing paperwork and holding the phone on one ear (a real Type A!). Suddenly I felt a pain in the center of my chest. Thinking I had something caught in my throat, I made several trips to the water fountain. After a few minutes, I realized what was happening, so I asked my secretary to walk me across the street to the Emergency Room (she told me later that was "The longest walk I ever had in my life!"). Within a few hours, I was evaluated, taken for a cardiac catheterization, and underwent a successful angioplasty to open a blocked coronary artery. (There were no "stents" in those days.)

As I reflected on that ordeal and my several months of recovery, I realized that God had certainly attracted my attention in a new and deeper way. It started in the E.R., where I experienced fear, embarrassment, and anxiety of the highest order. Yet the calm reassurance of my wife and brother, and a brief phone call from the hospital chaplain, seemed to say, "I am with you." It continued in the catheterization lab, where my cardiologist said it had been one of the "quickest, slickest" procedures of that type he had ever seen. Three weeks later, he called me at home, not once, but several times, to tell me how "spectacular" the results of a test had been, indicating that heart damage had not been extensive. He even used the words "almost miraculous."

I smiled as I walked around my yard after his call, and thought of the many people in my life (family, friends, and colleagues) who were praying for me. I praised and thanked God for them. I was overwhelmed with flowers, plants, gifts, visitors, and calls from friends and family. Feeling unworthy of that outpouring of love, I cried on several occasions.

One unforgettable visitor was a friend named "Katie" who sat with me quietly one afternoon. She asked me what I thought God was teaching me through my situation. I said, "Courage, patience, and to be less aggressive and ambitious." Katie smiled in her calm and peaceful way and added, "And to learn how to accept other people's love."

On a card from my graduate advisor of 20 years before, that distinguished professor inscribed, "Having survived your M.I. (myocardial infarction), God has your attention and I know that you will heed the message!.... Please do care for yourself; you are very important to all those who love you."

My Dean, a devout Jewish man, not only covered for me at work and made the long drive to visit me at home several times, but continued to counsel me like an older brother, "Seek help from a higher power." Meanwhile, my family motivated me to continue the regimen of diet, medications, and exercise via the O.S.U. Cardiac Rehab Program.

The people I met through the cardiac rehab program were friendly, welcoming, and supportive. From my first day there, when I felt angry, scared, and apprehensive, the nurses and participants became caring and understanding friends. The benefits were physical and psychological as we shared greetings, jokes, birthday/anniversary announcements, and family news. After ten years in the program, we were designated "The Ten of Hearts Club."

God's love through all these people gave me a new strength to change my behavior pattern and to *trust* as I grew closer to Him. I came to realize that it took a heart attack for God to get my attention.

✝

Milestones
(People and Programs)

Along my journey, certain people and programs have been "milestones" that directed my path professionally, personally, and spiritually. As I look back, I realize that I have been truly blessed to have had wonderful teachers, mentors, and role models.

In September, 1975, Elaine and I made our first "Marriage Encounter" weekend. We learned that the weekend, in spite of its name, was not a *confrontation*, but an intimate sharing with our spouse, a new "discovery" of our lives together.

It was a spiritual awakening for both of us, and a significant turning point in our lives. One of its tenets was "*Love is a decision.*" As "team" couples shared their marriage joys and sorrows and described how they prayerfully enriched their unions, we were inspired to review and renew our commitment to one another. Marriage Encounter clearly contributed to our renewed ministry to one another and to our parish. Shortly after our first weekend, we attended a "deeper" weekend called "Retorno," and eventually we served on "team" for a number of weekends.

For years, we met with M.E. couples from the West side of Columbus for monthly gatherings called "I.M.A.G.E." (an acronym for "I, Marriage and God Encounter"). There, we shared in confidence the successes and difficulties of our married lives together. I am close friends with these couples to this day.

Marriage Encounter Couples

Years later, our M.E. experience aided us in preparing engaged couples for marriage. I especially remember one young groom-to-be asking us, "O.K., what's the secret; in one word, what's the secret to your marriage of 50+ years?" I thought for a moment and said, "Tolerance." Elaine answered, "Patience."

In September and October of 1984, we made the "Cursillo" weekend (now ecumenical and called "Cum Christo" in Columbus). Again, we were deeply and spiritually enriched by this three day program of talks presented by ten lay persons and three "Spiritual Directors." Even though we attended separate weekends (males and females), we each made new commitments to Christ, realizing that we are His hands and feet and lips in this world.

For years, and continuing to this day, we meet and share weekly (called "grouping") with other "Cursillistas," following an outline of "piety, study, and action" that is the basis of the Cursillo movement. Our grouping with fellow Christians is a solid source of comfort and support as we encounter the joys, sorrows, trials, and tribulations that life presents.

In August.1988, eleven months after my heart attack, I sat down and wrote, for the first time in my life, my "GOALS." I categorized them as "spiritual," "personal," "professional," and "financial." I still have this list, and as I review it now, I realize how the Lord has helped me achieve most of them. One of my "spiritual" goals at that time was to pursue the diaconate.

Ordination Februrary 1, 1997

My ordination as a Catholic deacon in February, 1997 was certainly one of the major spiritual experiences of my life. My call to service may have started in second grade when I was an altar boy; even then I had the thought that maybe God was calling me to be a priest. But other "priorities" seemed to intervene, like the "discovery" of girls in Junior High School.

On one occasion during my early married life, my parish priest arrived at Mass with laryngitis, and asked me to proclaim some of the priest's readings that were part of the Mass. At the Gospel, I asked for his blessing, as I had seen ordained deacons do, and did my best to proclaim the Gospel. I was happy that he did not expect me to give a homily; he omitted it that day. I now see that event as a precursor to my diaconal calling.

My ministries as lector and Extraordinary Minister of the Eucharist led me to actively pursue more information on the diaconate in the late 1980's. My heart attack in September, 1987 had directed my attention more toward God and caused me to ponder my mortality. I felt called to learn more about this "new" clergy, so I interviewed with the director of the diaconate, who gave me brochures and directed me to apply to the two-year preparatory program in lay ministry called "C.H.R.I.S.M." (acronym for "Christians Respond in Shared Ministry"). That program for both males and females was required for males interested in applying to the diaconate program.

He also directed me to a diaconal candidate working at O.S.U., in fact, just across the street from my building. As I talked to "Phil," I noticed a Western New York accent, and asked if he was from Buffalo. He verified that he was. We discovered that he had grown up on a side street called "Woodside," off South Park Avenue, right around the corner from my house on South Park! I took that as a sign that I should continue to pursue the diaconate. Elaine and I attended Phil's ordination in 1990, and we have been good "compare" ever since.

For two years (1989-90), I car-pooled to "Abba House," a former retreat center in South Columbus, with another gentleman interested in the diaconate. We attended classes, completed assigned readings and papers, and had interesting class discussions about lay ministry. The program was excellent preparation for later courses in the seminary.

In 1991, I applied for the diaconate, completing an exhaustive set of documents and providing Baptismal and Confirmation records, letters of recommendation, etc. However, we were soon disappointed to learn that the bishop had decided to re-evaluate the diaconate program. We waited almost two years, and were eventually invited to resubmit new applications. We were interviewed in our home by a deacon and his wife, and finally I was admitted to the three year program of studies at the Josephinum Seminary. The rigorous program was equivalent to a Master's degree and included course work, papers, and "practicums" (workshops) on each aspect of a deacon's ministry. Our wives were invited but not required to sit in on our classes. Our class of twelve progressed yearly through the ministries of "Lector" and "Acolyte," which are steps on the way to ordination as "deacon."

On our 30th wedding anniversary in 1996, Elaine and I left for a 19-day group trip to Italy. It was a wonderful experience during which time we left our tour group twice, once to take a side trip to Soveria Mannelli in Calabria, my father's birthplace, and once to visit Bagheria, Sicily, my mother's birthplace. In Soveria, we stayed overnight with Ida Perri, a "cumare" from South Buffalo who had retired to Italy several yeas earlier. Her son Gabriel had been my Confirmation sponsor when I was in seventh grade. In Bagheria, we saw the Catholic Church where my mother was likely baptized, but it was locked and we could not enter. We almost missed the departure of our group from Palermo, Sicily, as they were leaving for Rome for our return flight to the U.S.A.

I fondly recall the dramatic ceremony of Ordination on February 1, 1997, when the Bishop Griffin firmly placed his hands on my head and said the words of ordination. I felt that it was Christ Himself calling me to His service. As I look back on my twenty-three years as a deacon, it has truly been a labor of love. It is a joy to serve in the three diaconal ministries of Liturgy, Word, and Charity.

My "Liturgical" ministry consists of assisting at Mass and presiding for baptisms (four of which have been my grandchildren), weddings, funeral services, and holy hours. My "Word" ministries have been preaching, teaching, and training lectors, ministers of the Eucharist, altar servers, and usher/greeters. "Charity" functions have included serving at an inner city soup kitchen and distributing food, clothing, and household items to inner city agencies.

One particular Baptism is very memorable. I was summoned at 11:00 P.M. one night to O.S.U. hospital, to the N.I.C.U. area, to baptize the premature baby girl of a young dental student and his wife. Seeing this tiny baby in critical condition in an incubator, I asked the nurse, "How can I pour water over this baby to baptize her?" She said, "Use an eyedropper." Gloved and gowned, I reached into the incubator and holding this tiny baby in one hand, said the prayers of Baptism, "I baptize you…" That baby survived, and to this day, some twenty years later, I still get a Christmas card and update from this young lady now living in Colorado.

One sad but memorable funeral was for my great niece who died in Buffalo at the age of five from a brain tumor. Little "Rita Rose" had trouble seeing the blackboard on her first day of kindergarten, and subsequent tests revealed the tumor. She underwent several surgeries but eventually succumbed to the disease. It was one of the most painful experiences of my ministry.

In 2001, my son and I traveled to Honduras with a group of volunteers to help construct a hospice for children with A.I.D.S. In subsequent years, I travelled to Bay St. Louis, Mississippi to do reconstruction work after hurricane Katrina and to Joplin, Missouri after tornadoes hit there.

At this writing, only three of my diaconate classmates are active in ministry in Central Ohio. Four have passed on, two have retired from the diaconate, and three others are out of state. Two of us are widowers. My closeness to my classmates continues through meetings, Emails, "Facetime" contacts, texts, and phone calls. We support one another through illnesses, surgeries, family crises, and bereavements. These classmates and their families, as well as all my deacon brothers, have truly been a blessing on my journey.

✝

Dad, Dean, and Deacon (Multiple Roles)

My life as Dad, Dean, and Deacon became more complicated as time went on. In 1983, while I was Assistant Dean in the College, we had our fourth child, a son, born nine years after our third daughter. While I believe that there is a very special relationship between a father and his daughter(s), I think that most men want a son, if it be God's will, not only to carry on the family name, but someone of the same gender to identify with. Therein lies the story of "Anthony G.'s" birth. The "G" stands for George, my Dad's first name, because he's very much a part of this story.

My Dad, George Edward "Papa" Morrison, had the opportunity to legally adopt my sister Carol and me when he married our mother in 1948. Had he done so, we would have taken the "Morrison" surname. This generous man chose not to force his family name upon me because "Some day, Tony may have a boy, and he would want him to carry on his father's name." (He assumed that Carol's name would change upon her marriage). He and our mother eventually had three more children, two girls and a boy. We have always treated each other as brothers and sisters, not as "half-brother" or "half-sister."

Papa couldn't have guessed that after thirty-five years, a boy would eventually be part of the Lord's great plan. Our girls had been praying for a baby brother, so they were delighted when I called them at school and gave them the good news. When Papa came to visit us a few weeks later, he said, "Now your family is complete – God gave you your boy." And my dear Mom, then seven years in heaven, and recalling my father's joy when I was born, smiled upon us, shed a few tears of joy, and turned to thank God for His goodness.

During my "Dad" days, I would sometimes come home from work, let loose a long sigh, and say to my dear wife, "Life is just getting too complicated – at work, at home, and in our social activities. How do we cope?" My kind and patient wife would look at me with sympathetic eyes and try to say something soothing.

My marriage, fatherhood, and relocation all commenced within the year before I started graduate school. In my first two career positions, I was expected to contribute to my profession; yet at the same time, I expected myself to be the best husband, father, neighbor, and church leader.

Many professional relationships developed from the travelling seminar program, and many personal relationships developed from Marriage Encounter, Cursillo, and other church and school activities. Several children and several complexities later, a whole new set of complexities set in: children going off to college; concerns about their career, courses, and costs; more and more high school activities; all while raising elementary and pre-school children, and often times, caring for elderly parents.

At the same time, our profession was going through complex changes at high speed. The volume of professional reading material multiplied; organizations and seminars vied for time, attention, and money, and the pressure to contribute to the literature and practice continued.

I often felt that I was living two lives – one out in the world and one at home. Sometimes I had to stop and think which hat I was wearing, or which set of clothes.

Once, when I was going through a difficult time of worry and uncertainty about the future, my Dad told me a personal true story with deep meaning. In 1964, he had made a trip back to see the farm in Cape Briton, Nova Scotia, Canada, where he was born and raised. He walked through the fields down to the stream where he had fished as a boy. There he sat on the same big rock he had sat on as a youngster. As he sat alone in the peace and tranquility of the country, he watched the stream, flowing slowly and steadily by.

Papa's Story

He thought of all he had been through in his lifetime: leaving school at the sixth grade level because he was needed to work on the farm and in the woods to help support a family of eleven children; losing a brother in a terrible barn fire; leaving home and joining the Canadian Army at the age of 28 when the war broke out; crawling on his belly over several countries in Europe, looking for land mines with a bayonet; immigrating to the United States in 1947, and marrying a widow with two small children; laboring in a steel plant to support his family, then with five children; being nearly killed and totally disabled in 1957 as the result of a terrible accident at the steel plant; watching his wife and children run a little store to sustain ourselves (barely) through elementary and high school...

He continued to watch the calm stream, still flowing under God's hand, slowly and imperturbably. And he thought, no matter where he had been or who he might have become, in spite of all he had been through, all the worries, anxieties, troubles and uncertainties of his lifetime, the stream still flowed. God had sustained him as He had sustained that stream. The world went on under His perfect control.

And so, my Dad calmly advised me to have faith and always remember this little story in the midst of hardships, troubles, worries, and anxieties. *"Don't forget,"* he said, *"The stream'll still be flowin'."* His story was published in *Marriage Encounter* magazine in December, 1977.

In 1986, I authored a "Commentary" which was published in the *American Journal of Hospital Pharmacy* entitled *"Living With Complexity."* In it, I outlined the growing complexity in my personal and professional life, including the complexities in the delivery of health care, technology, and manpower. I discussed the complexity of the health care marketplace, intra-professional rivalry, and legislative and ethical considerations. Finally, I tried to identify the future needs of my profession in order to cope with these complexities.

I eventually came to the conclusion that complexity is part of life. Life *should* be active, challenging, and exciting. The more we try to simplify things, the more we get involved in new things. Indeed, perhaps life's greatest challenge is to strike a *balance* between our work life, home life, religious life, and social life. As a close colleague once said, "Life wasn't meant to be easy!"

A well-known Franciscan priest at Steubenville once said, "Christianity is highly inconvenient!" As we study the scriptures, we discover that Jesus is gentle, but Jesus is demanding. He asks us to join our sufferings with His. At times like this, we may ask,

"How do we handle the everyday stuff, and yet keep God first in our life?

There once was a frail but wise old man in Rome with some suggestions. In one of his last encyclicals, Pope St. John Paul II said, *"Be docile to the movement of the Holy Spirit; learn the art of prayer; make the Eucharist the center of your parish life."*

Many years ago, when I was grieving the loss of a relative, a priest friend told me, "Always remember, our whole purpose for being here is to return to God." Indeed, growth (life) is a complex process; it is God's divine plan for us to return to Him.

My life as Assistant Dean became more difficult when the Dean I had worked with for eleven years decided to return to the faculty to teach and continue his cancer research. The new Dean was less than understanding about my need to continue in the cardiac rehabilitation program. I worked extra hours early in the morning and evenings, and weekends at home, to more than make up for the three or four hours per week that I attended the program.

"It's not fair!" I said to my friend Phil as we walked on campus one day. As I pointed out all the new guy's faults as I perceived them, I said, "Why did God bring this person into my life right now?!" My friend listened to my tirade patiently, occasionally offering, "a-huh...um-hum." When I stopped, he thought for a moment and said, "Tony, did you ever consider that maybe God brought *you* into *his* life?" I'm not sure I understood him then, but over the years, I've come to learn that "God's ways are not our ways."

Unexpectedly, about one year after I began my diaconate studies at the Josephinum, the university offered an "E.R.I.P." (Early Retirement Incentive Program). For anyone who had at least 25 years of service, the university would "buy" the person five more years credit and put them over the thirty years needed for retirement. Fortunately, because I had kept my part-time faculty appointment while at Mount Carmel Medical Center and had also taught a pharmacy lab at Buffalo, I had 26.5 years service credit. I discussed the offer with my family, friends, and cardiologist, and decided to accept the offer. I applied for and received an "Emeritus" title, which allowed me to continue to use university facilities such as the library and exercise areas.

When I was first interviewed for the diaconate in 1992, I remember the deacon who interviewed me saying, "Well, I don't see how you can carry on your work responsibilities and diaconate duties at the same time!" (I was sure he would not recommend me for the program.) But God had a plan for me to retire early and complete my diaconate studies.

✝

Birth to Death
(The role of Prayer)

My prayer life has certainly grown over the years. As a young married man, I didn't see my role as the spiritual leader for my family. We attended church strictly as a Sunday obligation, and were "Punch in, punch out, give me my wafer and let me go home" Catholics.

As Elaine and I got involved with Parish and Diocesan Councils, a guitar choir, a scripture study group called "Serendipity," C.C.D., lectoring, distributing the Eucharist, and taking Communion to the sick, God was gently preparing us for several challenges in the years that followed.

Oswald Chambers wrote: "We tend to use prayer as a last resort, but God wants it to be our first line of defense. We pray when there's nothing else we can do, but God wants us to pray before we do anything at all."

Personally, I went from memorized, "rote" prayer more toward "extemporaneous" prayer, i.e., prayer in my own words. In the early 70's, I was invited to attend a Saturday morning men's scripture group at the Baptist church across the road from my home. I was the only Catholic there, and I felt incompetent in explaining or defending the Catholic faith among men who were Methodist, Presbyterian, Mennonite, and Baptist. But the men were welcoming and respectful of each other's faith traditions; they tried to emphasize our similarities and accept our differences. We even went on a retreat together, praying, singing, and enjoying fellowship together.

One Saturday morning when Elaine and I were expecting our fourth child, the men surprised me with a "baby shower," presenting me with only "boy" gifts! At that time, we didn't know that God had a baby boy in our future, but the men apparently believed that would be the case. The local newspaper even picked up the story.

Over the years, I developed my early morning routine of bible reading and the reading of "daily devotionals." Morning was my best time for prayer, before the children got up for school, whereas late evening was Elaine's best time, after the children went to bed.

We mourned the passing of my mother in 1977, and Elaine's mother in 1984. We had moved her mother to Plain City in 1980, the same year that my brother Dennis got married and moved to Columbus to attend Capital Law School.

After courageously supporting my mother through her five year battle with cancer, my Dad accepted her death in 1977 as God's will without any bitterness. At the time, he said to my younger brother, "We will never get over this, but we will learn to live with it."

He tried living alone for a while, but after his several bouts with depression, my siblings and I decided that he needed to live with family for his own physical and mental health. We devised a plan whereby he "rotated" to live in each of our five homes every few months. That went on for over ten years, with Dad accepting and enjoying living with his children and grandchildren. He knew all our neighbors and took walks every day through our neighborhoods. An avid reader, he would go through the daily newspaper "backwards and forwards," as he would say. Sometimes, reacting to the negative news of the day, he would say, "The whole world's gone mad!" Other times he would say, "Most of what you worry about doesn't happen." We still laugh when we remember his famous line when he would spot a dessert, saying, "That pie (cake, cookie, etc.) is winking at me."

In 1994, while living with my sister, he had private-duty nurses assisting him. The first nurse who came was named "Faith." Soon after, my sister received the weekly schedule of nurses who would be caring for him each day. The second nurse's name was "Teddy" (Papa's nickname). My sister was overwhelmed with a sense of God's presence as the weekly schedule read: "Faith-Teddy-Faith-Teddy-Faith-Teddy-Teddy."

Dad passed on peacefully at the age of 92 in 2004, having led a long and distinguished life. Because of his own short education, he always stressed the importance of education to his children and grandchildren. At the time of his passing, he had eleven grandchildren and nine great-grandchildren. His bedtime ritual included the words, "Good night, good luck, and God bless." To this day, I recite the rosary when I go to bed, using my Dad's well-worn "bed rosary," the kind with the large beads.

I am a "doer" by nature, and always use "to do" lists. I read books on organizing and prioritizing tasks, but always seem to revert to my "Type A" behavior. Now, when I feel that I am failing if I cannot accomplish everything on my list, I try to remember that the only important thing is that God is accomplishing *His* plan in my life.

While it is true that "prayer changes things," prayer doesn't change God; it changes the person who prays.

✝

Passing of a Spouse
(53 Years)

On July 19, 2018, the 70th anniversary of my parents' marriage, my wife Elaine was diagnosed with Stage IV lung cancer. It was a devastating blow to all of us, as she had never smoked nor drank. It was called "ROS-1," a rare lung cancer that, while not painful, affected her breathing. Her only symptoms leading up to the diagnosis was a persistent cough and shortness of breath since the previous Winter.   Over the next year, she was hospitalized eight times at the James Cancer Hospital at O.S.U., and was treated with two oral medications that prolonged her life but could not cure the cancer. She never complained about the diagnosis, making many trips to the hospital for out-patient checkups while continuing her service to the church almost to the end. I remember the last time she lectored, about two weeks before she passed. I

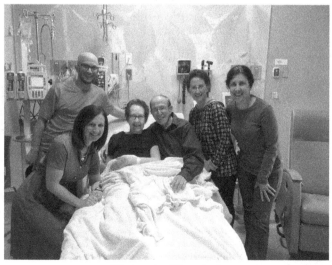

Elaine in Hospital

whispered to my pastor sitting beside me on the altar, "There goes a very brave woman."

On July 1, 2019, my 76th birthday, she insisted we travel to Buffalo "to see everyone." While there, we visited my siblings, her brother, and her only living cousin. She had arranged to have lunch with several of her old high school friends, and had arranged to visit the house where she grew up. The lunch with her friends was enjoyable for her, and the occupants of her childhood home were most gracious to show us the remodeled house.

We celebrated July Fourth at my sister's home, and on Sunday, July 7, went to Mass at Our Lady of Victory Basilica in Lackawanna, followed by a visit to the graves of our parents at Holy Cross Cemetery. I think Elaine knew this would be her last trip to Buffalo, and she made the most of it.

On our way back to Columbus, she agreed that we could stop in Cleveland for a brief visit with one of my graduate school classmates who was recovering from surgery for oral cancer. That was typical of her loving care for other people.

The next morning, July 8, I left her on the couch at home while I went to the YMCA to exercise. We were supposed to go in for a routine blood draw that morning, but when I returned from the Y, she said she was too weak, and that I should call her doctor to cancel. Based on her symptoms, they asked us to bring her in to the E.R. She was admitted to the James Hospital for the eighth time and spent the next five days there. On Friday, July 12, the 42nd anniversary of my mother's passing, the staff said we should consider "comfort care," i.e., hospice care. We decided to take her to Kobacker House, a respected hospice near the campus.

We took her there that evening, and she slowly regressed over the next 48 hours. The staff made her as comfortable as possible. She had limited visitors including family and a few close friends. One of our previous pastors, who Elaine had served as Director of Religious Education, came and blessed her on Saturday. She passed peacefully at 11:00p.m. on Sunday evening, July 14, 2019, our oldest daughter's 52nd birthday, and just five days short of her one-year-ago diagnosis.

During her two days at Kobacker House, Elaine had visions that she verbalized and comments that described what she was experiencing. I present them here for the reader to ponder. (She was speaking to our daughters Maria and Tina).

"Elaine's Glimpse of Heaven"

Quotes from July 11, 2019

"If I can't find him, will he find me?"

(Who, Mom?)

"Jesus! If I can't find him, will he find me?"

(Absolutely, Mom! He knows exactly where you are!)

"Has everyone been notified?"

(That you're in the hospital? Yes, Mom. What do you want me to let them know.)

"Tell them I'm taking off. "

(Where are you going? On vacation?)

"Heaven, I gotta go to Heaven."

(They're going to love you up there, Mom.")

"I need to go to Heaven."

Quotes from July 12, 2019

"What a beautiful death. It couldn't be more beautiful."
"There's Papa! Hi Papa! Look at that haircut Papa has! It's nice!"

"Hi God, glad to meet you. Very glad to meet you! What have you got waiting for me to do?"

"Look at that lady dancing. These decorations are beautiful."

"Are you an angel?"

(No, Mom, it's just me.)
"I see an angel in your face. I'm not dead yet? I thought I was in Heaven."

"I see a little girl, and she's waving at me."

"Let's get this show on the road!"

At the visitation before her funeral, we made copies of this document available, and have since distributed many more copies. She had written her own obituary, but had chosen not to have a video playing during the visitation, so we laid out some of her teaching materials and memorabilia for people to peruse. Her funeral took place on Thursday, July 18 at Saint Joseph Church in Plain City, where we had been parishioners for 48 years. Three priests concelebrated and about twenty of my brother deacons attended. The Director of the Diaconate and my Buffalo friend Deacon Phil assisted on the altar. It was a beautiful and moving ceremony with the church overflowing such that some people had to watch it being live-streamed to the Parish Activity Center.

Elaine had told me that she wanted to be interred in Buffalo in the Bonacci family plot, so we took her there on Friday, July 19, and interred her on Saturday, July 20. I was privileged to conduct the Rite of Committal at the graveside. My biological father Carmen and my uncle Frank are buried there, and there is one more space for me.

Elaine chose to have any memorial donations made to our Parish Building Fund. Over $25,000 was donated in her memory, including her own donation from her I.R.A. One of the windows in the church was dedicated to her memory just before Christmas of 2019.

To lose a spouse of 53 years is a heart-breaking, difficult cross to bear, but I know for sure where she is, in the care of Our Lord, with all our family and friends who have passed on before us. I pray that she prepares a place for us.

Since Elaine's passing, I have received many expressions of sympathy and support from family, friends, neighbors, and colleagues. Many have generously assisted me with necessary chores both indoors and outside. One Saturday morning, about twelve cars showed up in my driveway; my brother Knights of Columbus came to trim trees and shrubs and haul away the debris. Overwhelmed by their generosity, I cried.

In the months that followed, I tried to "stay busy," and that's what I told people who asked, "How are you doing?" I read several books on being a widower, (including one book personally signed by the author, sent to me graciously by a former classmate in graduate school), but told family and friends, "I never thought in a million years that I would be a widower!" I had prepared my funeral plans, as required by the diocese, and had spelled out all matters relating to our personal business in a folder. My will was updated, and I had shown Elaine where everything was, fully expecting that I would pass first. I gave her clear directions on where everything was, even including the safe deposit box key. After all, I was the one with coronary artery disease! But God had other plans.

I continued my ministry as best I could, but missed my spouse terribly. There were times of uncontrolled sobbing, especially evenings and nights. At times, I said, "Elaine, why did you leave me?" When I would sit in my chair or in the car, I missed her sitting beside me.

I formed a "Widowers' Group" in my parish and invited several widowed men from neighboring parishes as well. It was not meant to be a scripture study group, but rather a support group where we could share our thoughts, feelings, and coping mechanisms in confidence. I photo-copied and distributed helpful materials from the internet and from several hospice organizations. Our group of seven men met monthly until the "COVID" virus hit. Our group consisted of men who had been widowed for only a few years of marriage, to one 92-year old man who had been widowed after 61 years of marriage! It was a diverse group of Catholics and non-

Catholics. As of this writing, we have not been able to reconvene due to the Coronavirus and "spacing" guidelines.

I have heard all my life, "The good die young." Truly, Elaine was a patient, loving person who always put the other person's welfare ahead of her own. She was a Brownie and Girl Scout leader when our girls were growing up, a memory they surely cherish. Elaine served as a religion teacher in our parish for over thirty years, and as a fourth grade elementary school teacher for ten years.. She also volunteered at the Dublin Methodist hospital in Pastoral Care for over ten years, ever since that facility opened.

Clearing out her closet and going through her personal items such as jewelry, books, and computer files, has been painful. I donated most of her clothes to a local women's prison, as they give each inmate a few sets of clothes when they are released. Elaine had a large number of head scarves she had worn as her hair thinned. I distributed them to the parish ladies of the "Walking With Purpose" bible study group which she had helped to organize. I'm sure she would be happy to see them wearing her scarves in memory of her.

Ladies of Saint Joseph Wearing Elaine's Scarves

Saint Joseph the Worker Parish ("Saint's Alive")

We moved into our home South of Plain City on September 12, 1971 and promptly began attending Saint Joseph parish. A priest of the Precious Blood order, which had founded the parish in 1884 (by priests riding out to Plain City on horseback from Columbus), was the pastor. However, we did not feel welcome there and soon searched for another parish.

At the time, Sts. Simon and Jude parish in West Jefferson was staffed by a priest of the Oblates of Mary Immaculate (O.M.I.) order. That order of priests offers themselves to the service of God with Mary as their model.

The pastor there told stories of his service as a missionary in Africa, and every Mass began or ended with the hymn, "Immaculate Mary." Now, that hymn recalls memories of that dedicated pastor and his devotion to Mary, as well as his homily every Mother's Day. He would forcefully say, "You mothers, don't you dare hang your head and say, 'I'm only a homemaker…' Be proud! – motherhood is the most noble profession there is!"

We soon made friends there, and joined the newly formed guitar choir (that was quite the thing in the 70's!). One family started a home-based bible study group, and we soon became involved in other ministries such as lectoring and communion to the sick.

We returned to Saint Joseph when "Father Steve" became pastor. The story was that when he rode into Plain City on his motorcycle (with his long hair), several teachers we knew were sitting on their front porch on North Chillicothe Street and said, "Well, there goes the neighborhood!" But Father Steve was a gentle, loving and caring priest who enamored himself to all. We'll never forget when he was to leave the parish and he stayed up all night composing a song to sing and play on his guitar at his last Mass with us. I still

St. Joseph Church

have it on tape.

He was followed by "Father Ray," who did his best to implement the dictates of Vatican II, even though he found it difficult. During this time, I spoke many times with our first deacon, Rev. Mr. Robert Stock, about the diaconate. Bob had been ordained in 1985, and he was very supportive of my interest in becoming a deacon. Sadly, he passed at Easter time in 1991 from prostate cancer, having served for only six years as a deacon.

"Father Blu" was next, serving only two years. He used to admit to us, "I want you to know, I'm taking one dollar out of the collection each week and buying a lottery ticket, and if we win, we're building a new church." No one objected.

He was followed by "Father Charlie," who I consulted about my interest in becoming a deacon. He supported me and agreed that I should enter the C.H.R.I.S.M. ("Christians Respond in Shared Ministry") program, the lay ministry formation program which was a necessary pre-requisite for my application to the diaconate.

"Father Kevin" was my mentor from 1991-1996 before moving on to Holy Family parish in the inner city, where he founded the "Jubilee Museum," the largest collection of Catholic artifacts in the country. While at St. Joseph, he often took me with him to Children's Hospital, where he served as Chaplain.

My formal training program at the Josephinum extended from 1994-1996. It was during this time, in 1995, that "Father Gabriel," a friend of Father Kevin's from Tanzania, came to our parish for the summer.

One Thursday morning, Jeanie Martin, a parishioner, took Father Gabriel and I to the Holy Family Soup Kitchen. One experience there, and I was "hooked." For the next ten years or so, I served as the "head cook" every Thursday morning, volunteering with five or six others to prepare and serve a hot meal to needy persons of the inner city.

When we opened the doors of the soup kitchen to let the people in, Jeanie would smile and say, "Here comes Jesus!" She taught us by her example that loving service to those in need is service given to Christ Himself.

As the former bishop of Columbus once said to our *confirmandi*, "The first time Jesus came, He came as a babe; will we recognize

Him when He comes again? Learn to recognize Him in the faces of those in need."

"Father Francis," the pastor at Holy Family, would often help us serve the folks, and he liked to say, "Tony, this isn't a soup kitchen; this is a restaurant!" (because the food was of such good quality). He had founded the soup kitchen many years before, and it ran like a well-oiled machine, because he had arranged for food donations from parishes, restaurants, banquet halls, and Mount Carmel Hospital. We were never short of food to serve at least 100 people daily.

"Father Pat," a staunch Irishman, served Saint Joseph parish for the next 18 years, from 1997 to 2015, while also serving as a military chaplain for the Air Force. When he was away on duty, several of his priest friends would celebrate the Masses, including "Father Tom" and "Father Ralph." These were good opportunities for me to experience assisting other priests at Mass and other liturgies.

Just before Christmas of 1998, I experienced the presence of a "Christmas angel." I had been admitted to O.S.U. hospital through the E.R. after fainting at home. When I arrived at my room, my young roommate gave a little smile as I introduced myself, but was otherwise very private. I asked his name, and he said simply, "John." When I asked him what brought him into the hospital, he said, "diabetes." When I inquired about family, he said, "Oh, they're here somewhere…" (I found out later that he had not had even one visitor even though he had been there three and one half weeks). When I asked what kind of work he did, he chuckled and said simply, "construction."

I couldn't help overhearing his conversation with a social worker when she said she was "getting him some medications and diabetic supplies to last him for a while, and some information on organizations for the homeless." She said he would be discharged the next day. All day the next day, he kept saying his "friend" would come by and pick him up, but he seemed to be stalling. (It was a cold, snowy day outside.) While he was in the bathroom, I asked the nurse, "Does he have a place to go; does he have any money?" She said she didn't know, but her sympathetic look said she did know.

As it got dark, I heard him call a cab, and I decided to offer him some cash when he left. I was on the phone with my sister when all of a sudden, he drew back the drapes and bolted out the door, wearing only a tee shirt and jeans, and with no suitcase. I called out to him, "Hey, John," as I fumbled for my wallet; I thought I would slip him at least a twenty dollar bill. That's when the strangest thing happened. John kept right on going, giving me a little smile over his shoulder, and waving at me with the back of his hand. I heard a quick, "Bye," and he was gone.

When I told my sister what had just happened, she said, "Maybe John was your Christmas angel, and maybe his work was done." Maybe he was, because the next morning the doctor said, "You know that blood draw we did last night? Well, your lab values have started to turn around; you've turned the corner!" So was it a "coincidence?" Or was John on a mission?

Our Knights of Columbus Council # 12772 was formed in 2000, and has served the parish well. I am proud to be a "Charter member," and served as "Grand Knight" in 2005-2006. Over the years, the Knights have conducted many events such as Lenten fish frys which have enabled them to sponsor college scholarships, several seminarians' needs, and needed items for the parish such as priest and deacon vestments.

The parishioners of St. Joseph completed and happily dedicated the "Parish Activity Center" (P.A.C.) in 2006. Within a few years, it was entirely paid for. Elaine and I were to have our 40th wedding anniversary reception at the P.A.C. on June 18, 2006, but it wasn't finished in time, so we had to find another venue. It happened that the bishop came for Confirmation that day, and we rented the high school auditorium for that ceremony. I have a photo of the bishop giving Elaine and I an anniversary blessing on that special day.

During Father Pat's tenure, the parish hired an architect to plan a new church, and a Parish Building Fund was started. Parishioners made pledges, and hoped to raise 50% of the building cost so that construction could begin. Unfortunately, that did not happen, so contributions to our Parish Building Fund will continue until funds are sufficient to proceed.

In 2014, we celebrated our parish's "Sesqui-Centennial" (150 years since our founding); Elaine and I were delighted to serve as chairpersons for a year-long observance.

"Father Joe" arrived from Jackson, Ohio in 2015, and presently serves our parish of 350 families. He has made physical improvements at the P.A.C., and will be remembered for having the children hold up posters with key words as he presents his homilies.

Over the years, many lay people have made significant contributions to the life of the parish. For example, Wally Cooper (affectionately called "Monsignor Wally") will long be remembered as the parish Sacristan. Ed and Bonnie Chuha and Gloria and Jim Butler founded our "Martin dePorres Outreach Center," which supports and supplies needy families with emergency funds, furniture, and household articles. Joe Hofbauer, a village historian and active parishioner, served in many roles, including parish council member and parish photographer. Many ladies and gentlemen, too many to list, have served as religion teachers and Youth Ministers, and many have volunteered as lectors, ushers, altar servers, and Extraordinary Ministers of the Eucharist. Others set up and decorate the church for special holy days and special events. Indeed, we are a church of "Saints Alive," as Father Pat liked to call us.

Bishop Desmond Tutu once said, "We do not need to *prove* ourselves to God...we do not need to *impress* God, for God's love has taken the initiative..." We should strive to be God's instruments to pay our debts to God, in *thanksgiving* for God's many blessings.

As of this writing, I have completed my 23rd year as a deacon at Saint Joseph parish. Each priest I have served with has their own style and their own strengths. I have been able to get along pretty well with all of them.

An American Baptist pastor, once quoted in the *Catholic Digest*, said, "God has taken vessels like you and me-- marred and flawed as we are-- and used us in great and mighty ways." Sooner or later, we come to realize that God uses our strong points and our weak points to move us forward to achieve His plan. Sooner or later, we are willing and eager to be His instrument.

During my years as deacon, the bishop asked me on two occasions to serve as a temporary "Pastoral Administrator" at parishes which were between pastors or where the pastor was physically disabled. My experience as an Assistant Dean helped me to keep things running smoothly and efficiently.

✝

Preaching
(Making the Word Relevant)

I really enjoy preaching. Looking back, I now realize how my life experiences have prepared me for this part of my ministry. Perhaps it started in kindergarten, when "Mrs. McIntosh" trained me to be the "M.C." for a play we put on for our parents. I still remember nervously leading the audience in the "Pledge of Allegiance."

In elementary and high school, there were debate teams that argued topics of the day, and the "Model U.N.," in which "representatives" of various countries debated topics of international interest. These exercises were good training for public speaking. At Bishop Timon High School, I was a "brother" in the "History and Civics Fraternity," a group of students that taught and promoted public discourse on local and national topics.

In college and graduate school, we presented papers and essays in seminar courses to fellow classmen. For four years on the "Bag Show" (see chapter 9), I presented talks to hundreds of hospital pharmacists in various cities throughout the United States and Canada. As a professor in the College of Pharmacy, we "team taught" seniors in a Professional Practice course. My Assistant Dean duties included budget presentations to the Provost and President of the University.

As an Assistant Director of Pharmacy in the hospital, I trained pharmacy technicians in class and on the job. In my parish, lectoring (proclaiming the readings) gave me the opportunity to present God's Word to the assembly. At the Josephinum Seminary, we presented homilies to our fellow deacon candidates as part of a "practicum"(workshop).

I take my preaching ministry very seriously, spending many hours to prepare each homily. I still use an outlined procedure for preparing a homily that "Fr. Rod" gave us in his seminary course in "Homiletics."

The Word

One of the steps is to rehearse the homily (out loud) at home. In that regard, my wife Elaine was often my toughest critic. She would gently ask questions about the content or its meaning, and it always helped. For many years, I taped each homily and repeatedly played it back to self-assess my theme, timing, and delivery.

However, even though I know I'm well prepared, I still get nervous just before presenting a homily. I think it's the sense that I must do my best every time. As I raise the Book of the Gospels, I pray for the Holy Spirit to calm me and assist me.

My philosophy about preaching is that I must make the reading(s) *relevant* to the person sitting in the pew, now, *today*, wherever he (she) is in their faith journey. Our former bishop, Bishop James Griffin, in a lecture he once gave us in seminary, told us to *"...talk to the people where they are; challenge them and move them forward; challenge them without scolding; preach the gospel, not what's "popular" or "acceptable" currently in society; teach what the church teaches."*

My message must follow one clear theme that continues through the eight or nine minute (maximum) homily. It should be understandable to a junior high school student as well as the ninety year old senior, and relevant to single, widowed, and married persons alike. The homilist should keep in mind what is going on in the world as well as what's going on in his own life.

When I was in seminary, I recall reading a book called *"The I of the Sermon,"* in which the author recommended that the homilist should share something of *himself,* such as a story or true experience which relates to the theme of the message. He encouraged the homilist to be brave enough to risk sharing one's weaknesses or failings to demonstrate his humanness and vulnerability. In that regard, I try to start each homily with a true story from my past, but it must be one that directly relates to the theme of my homily. It can't be irrelevant or "forced."

In seminary, "Father Rod" taught us to *"...reach the people at their feeling level, their emotional level; get at their gut; use language that reaches their gut – not their head; talk about profound things simply; use simple words in profound ways."*

In 1998, as a "toddler" deacon of one year, I had an article published in *The Deacon Digest* entitled, *"Preaching – What the Congregation Wants."* In it, I stated that the congregation wants "spiritual nourishment" and "wants to know how they should act and think as Catholic Christians...our people want us to speak to them in a **spiritual** and **personal** way. They want witness – someone credible and worth listening to; and they want a voice that is pleasant, warm, and friendly."

Truly, there is a hunger for God in our people; they seek a deeper faith experience. It's the deacon's job to help them find Him in the Word when we preach. We must be compassionate and sympathetic, communicating that we are sensitive to their joys and sufferings. Our demeanor in presenting the homily should be gentle at times and bold at other times. It depends on the theme of the message and the Liturgical season.

I have found that the congregation is very "forgiving" in the event that the homilist loses his place, mispronounces a name, or errs in any way. This is especially true for the newly ordained deacon.

In many cases, the deacon is more approachable than the priest. For example, people have said to me, "You know what I'm going through with my teenager (wife, boss, etc.) because you've been there..." Or they may say, "You were speaking directly to me today; it's exactly what I've been going through...can we get together and talk about it?"

Our people deserve our best effort and should not stand for a poorly prepared, irrelevant, or disjointed homily. It is likely the only Word of God they will receive for the week. I believe strongly that people will attend worship services wherever they receive *spiritual nourishment*, including a well prepared and well delivered homily, and where they feel *welcome*.

✝

Communion of Saints
(The future)

As I approach my "octogenarian" birthday, I look back on all the blessings God has granted me, as well as the crosses that have benefitted me.

My M.I. in 1987 introduced me to a regimented exercise program and healthy diet which I continue to this day. The sequence of church activities and lay ministries spurred my spiritual growth and led me to the diaconate.

The loss of my biological father at an early age brought me a Dad who generously raised me like one of his own. His calm and faithful demeanor upon Mom's passing set an example for me to follow when my wife passed on.

The good Sisters of Mercy and Franciscan priests who taught me instilled a strong and firm Catholic faith which has sustained me through thick and thin.

The opportunity to be the first in my generation to get a college education and my dedicated mentors in graduate school enabled me to contribute to my fellow man through my profession. My colleagues in hospital practice and pharmaceutical research inspired me to strive for "the Big E," *enthusiasm*, and to use my God-given talents for the greater good.

My Italian heritage serves me well, as I continue its emphasis on "Faith, Family, and Food." I like to cook, host, and serve others. My emotional and sensitive personality is an asset in my ministry.

My wife of 53 years set an example for me of patient, loving concern for others before oneself. She was an excellent wife, parent, grandparent, teacher, and minister to others.

The people of Saint Joseph parish and my ministry as their Deacon has been the richest blessing of my life. The Baptisms, First Communions, Confirmations, weddings, funerals, and so many other occasions, are precious memories that time makes all the sweeter.

Recently, a preacher on the radio exhorted his listeners to *"Pray for revival; Prepare for survival; Watch for arrival."* At this tumultuous time in the Catholic Church, we need to pray for *revival.* The clerical sexual abuse problem has droned on since at least 2002. Administrative and financial malfeasance has plagued too many dioceses, and at this writing, at least 24 American dioceses, including my native Buffalo diocese, have declared bankruptcy due to payouts to sexual abuse victims and declining attendance in the parishes. Today, good bishops, priests, deacons and consecrated religious are challenged to restore trust in the Catholic Church. It may take some weeding, some pruning, some apologies, and the enactment of tough policies and procedures, but it will happen. I believe our Catholic Church will end up being leaner but stronger. As I have said to my pastor, "All we can do at our level is to be the best priest and deacon we can be for our local flock."

We need to prepare for *survival.* The COVID virus and the pandemic it has created threatens not only the elderly and those with chronic diseases, but has brought about financial insecurity for persons of all ages. *Spiritual revival* is also needed: moral relativism, materialism, secularism, and individualism threaten our way of life and the free practice of our faith.

Jesus wants us to watch for His *arrival.* He wants us to be alert for His second coming, and at the same time, to be prepared for the possibility of His calling us home first. In any case, prudent preparation is a matter of personal responsibility.

Some of us will have time to prepare, some won't. The end may seem far off. In the meantime, St. Matthew tells us that the deepest wisdom, the fullest readiness is living chastely, living honestly, and living non-violently [Matt.5] while meeting our neighbors' basic needs [Matt.25]. The book of Micah says, "…act justly, love mercy, and walk humbly with your God."[Micah 6:8] Sounds like a good plan!

My sister Joyce says that when we die and reach heaven, - that's when our eyes will REALLY see! We will be able to look back and think, "Oh, yeah, that's why that happened!"…Looking elsewhere in our life, "Oh yeah, Oh yeah, that's why…" God will let us see His plan in all His glory – how we were all connected and how we touched so many others, even by a simple smile, and how that helped them keep going until *they* reach heaven and get that "Oh, yeah…" moment for themselves.

May God bless you and yours…

My Siblings and I

About The Author

Deacon Anthony C. Bonacci is Assistant Dean Emeritus, College of Pharmacy, The Ohio State University. He is the father of four adult children, Lynn Marie (Chapman), Tina Marie (Hardin), Maria Margaret (Lentz), and Anthony G. Bonacci. Deacon Bonacci has been a member of Saint Joseph the Worker parish, Plain City, Ohio, for 49 years, and an ordained deacon for the Diocese of Columbus, Ohio, for 23 years.

He was married to his wife Elaine for 53 years until her untimely passing in 2019. Deacon Bonacci has eight grandchildren ranging in age from 29 years of age to five years of age. He has published articles in *Marriage Encounter* magazine, *Deacon Digest* magazine, *The Catholic Times* of Columbus, *The American Journal of Hospital Pharmacy*, *Tetrahedron Letters*, and local newsletters of the *Marriage Encounter* and *Cursillo* movements.

CPSIA information can be obtained
at www.ICGtesting.com
Printed in the USA
BVHW041205240321
603332BV00008B/1306